MATCH ANNUAL 2003

MATCH Editor > Simon Caney Art Director > Darryl Tooth Annual Editor > Ian Foster Assistant Editor > Kevin Hughes Production Editor > James Bandy Sub-Editor/Writers > Richard Adams, Kevin Pettman Staff Writer > Giles Milton Designers > Martin Barry, Calum Booth Staff Photographer > Phil Bagnall Cartoonist > Russ Carvell And the rest of the MATCH team > Becky Booth, Darren Cross, Dawn Brown & Glen Gregory

MATCH BRITAIN'S BIGGEST & BEST FOOTBALL MAGAZINE

Bushfield House, Orton Centre, Peterborough PE2 5UW ★ Tel: 01733 237111
Fax: 01733 288150 ★ e-mail: match.magazine@emap.com

>PLANET FOOTY!<

DID YOU KNOW?
Over 40 million footballs are sold worldwide every year! Are they to replace the ones kicked over fences into neighbours' gardens?

THE FAME GAME

From the cover of every newspaper and magazine, through endless multi-million pound advertising deals to telly channels devoted entirely to footy, football players are the new rock 'n' roll stars. But who's the biggest star in England? Planet Footy's taken a look at the candidates, looking at different aspects of the game to work it out. We've looked at their best footy moments, flashness, the amount of advertising they do, how much they appear in the newspapers, and how much they tend to show off. After that, we've come up with a verdict on who's the biggest star in England!

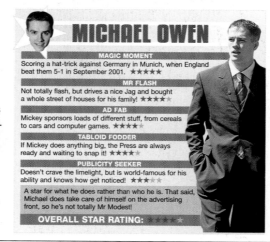

MICHAEL OWEN

MAGIC MOMENT
Scoring a hat-trick against Germany in Munich, when England beat them 5-1 in September 2001. ★★★★★

MR FLASH
Not totally flash, but drives a nice Jag and bought a whole street of houses for his family! ★★★★☆

AD FAB
Mickey sponsors loads of different stuff, from cereals to cars and computer games. ★★★★☆

TABLOID FODDER
If Mickey does anything big, the Press are always ready and waiting to snap it! ★★★☆☆

PUBLICITY SEEKER
Doesn't crave the limelight, but is world-famous for his ability and knows how get noticed! ★★★☆☆

A star for what he does rather than who he is. That said, Michael does take care of himself on the advertising front, so he's not totally Mr Modest!

OVERALL STAR RATING: ★★★★☆

DAVID BECKHAM

MAGIC MOMENT
A last minute free-kick against Greece last year to send England to the World Cup finals. ★★★★★

MR FLASH
If this guy was any more flash, he'd be a kitchen detergent. He's got a pop star wife, loadsa money and style! ★★★★★

AD FAB
Pepsi, Brylcreem, Police sunglasses – you name it, Becks is probably endorsing it. ★★★★★

TABLOID FODDER
If Becks opens a packet of crisps, a snapper will be there to catch it. A tabloid king. ★★★★★

PUBLICITY SEEKER
From his trendy haircut to demanding to take the penalty against Argentina, Becks loves it! ★★★★☆

A self-publicising, media-friendly manipulator of all things star-spangled and glamorous. The England skipper's not so much a star as a global icon!

STAR RATING: ★★★★.8

HIGH FIVE...

BEST CLUB SIDES IN THE WORLD 2002: Is your fave team one of the best in the world?

1. REAL MADRID
2. MAN. UNITED
3. BAYERN MUNICH
4. JUVENTUS
5. ARSENAL

RIO FERDINAND

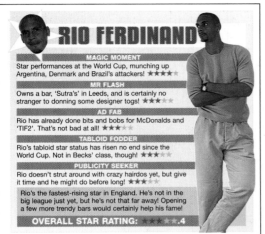

MAGIC MOMENT
Star performances at the World Cup, munching up Argentina, Denmark and Brazil's attackers! ★★★★★

MR FLASH
Owns a bar, 'Sutra's' in Leeds, and is certainly no stranger to donning some designer togs! ★★★★★

AD FAB
Rio has already done bits and bobs for McDonalds and 'TIF2'. That's not bad at all! ★★★★★

TABLOID FODDER
Rio's tabloid star status has risen no end since the World Cup. Not in Becks' class, though! ★★★★★

PUBLICITY SEEKER
Rio doesn't strut around with crazy hairdos yet, but give it time and he might do before long! ★★★★★

Rio's the fastest-rising star in England. He's not in the big league just yet, but he's not that far away! Opening a few more trendy bars would certainly help his fame!

OVERALL STAR RATING: ★★★★★.4

SOL CAMPBELL

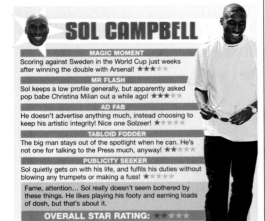

MAGIC MOMENT
Scoring against Sweden in the World Cup just weeks after winning the double with Arsenal! ★★★★★

MR FLASH
Sol keeps a low profile generally, but apparently asked pop babe Christina Milian out a while ago! ★★★★★

AD FAB
He doesn't advertise anything much, instead choosing to keep his artistic integrity! Nice one Solzeer! ★★★★★

TABLOID FODDER
The big man stays out of the spotlight when he can. He's not one for talking to the Press much, anyway! ★★★★★

PUBLICITY SEEKER
Sol quietly gets on with his life, and fulfils his duties without blowing any trumpets or making a fuss! ★★★★★

Fame, attention… Sol really doesn't seem bothered by these things. He likes playing his footy and earning loads of dosh, but that's about it.

OVERALL STAR RATING: ★★★★★

KIERON DYER

MAGIC MOMENT
His England debut against Luxembourg in 1999, where he had Wembley chanting his name! ★★★★★

MR FLASH
Fast cars, women, loads of dollar, holidays in Ayia Napa. Yeah, you could say Kieron's a bit flash! ★★★★★

AD FAB
The youngster's not really got into all that business yet. But his time will come… ★★★★★

TABLOID FODDER
Tales of Mr Dyer's exploits seem to pop up every week. Sir Bobby seems to have calmed that down, though! ★★★★★

PUBLICITY SEEKER
Kieron doesn't mean to get into all these little scrapes, they just seem to happen. Life ain't fair! ★★★★★

Kieron doesn't go out looking for attention or trouble – it goes out looking for him! The youngster's just a magnet to fame, but Bobby Robson's doing his best to keep him under control!

STAR RATING: ★★★★★.2

PAUL SCHOLES

MAGIC MOMENT
Two goals against Scotland at Hampden Park in the Euro 2000 play-off! ★★★★★

MR FLASH
No, not this bloke. Scholesy is Mr Unflash – probably the unflashiest man in the whole of footy! ★★★★★

AD FAB
No way! There are no advertising contracts in sight for the Ginger Ninja, other than his boot makers! ★★★★★

TABLOID FODDER
Scholes could go on a killing spree in Manchester and still get less press than Becks' new hairstyle. ★★★★★

PUBLICITY SEEKER
Not even slightly. Scholesy would much rather enjoy some peace and quiet away from the Press. ★★★★★

Scholesy isn't vaguely interested in the fame game, and the fame game isn't remotely interested in him either, so it's worked out pretty well all round.

STAR RATING: ★★★★★.6

THE PLANET FOOTY GUIDE TO USING YOUR 2003 ANNUAL

WITH USA COACH BRUCE ARENA!

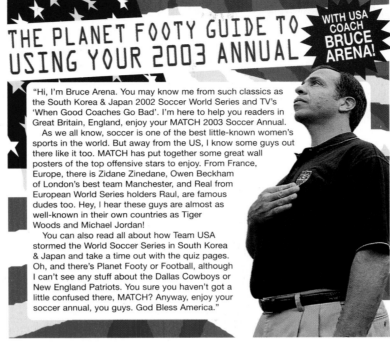

"Hi, I'm Bruce Arena. You may know me from such classics as the South Korea & Japan 2002 Soccer World Series and TV's 'When Good Coaches Go Bad'. I'm here to help you readers in Great Britain, England, enjoy your MATCH 2003 Soccer Annual.

As we all know, soccer is one of the best little-known women's sports in the world. But away from the US, I know some guys out there like it too. MATCH has put together some great wall posters of the top offensive stars to enjoy. From France, Europe, there is Zidane Zinedane, Owen Beckham of London's best team Manchester, and Real from European World Series holders Raul, are famous dudes too. Hey, I hear these guys are almost as well-known in their own countries as Tiger Woods and Michael Jordan!

You can also read all about how Team USA stormed the World Soccer Series in South Korea & Japan and take a time out with the quiz pages. Oh, and there's Planet Footy or Football, although I can't see any stuff about the Dallas Cowboys or New England Patriots. You sure you haven't got a little confused there, MATCH? Anyway, enjoy your soccer annual, you guys. God Bless America."

---

10 BRILLIANT WAYS TO BEAT MAN. UNITED!

1 Cut off the supply to Ruud van Nistelrooy!

2 Sit back and then hit them quickly on the counter-attack!

3 Hit the ball near Wes Brown when he's in front of his own goal!

4 Wind Roy Keane up so much that he gets sent-off!

5 Do your best to break David Beckham's metatarsal again!

6 Tell Fergie to play Laurent Blanc and Phil Nev in defence!

7 Let Juan Sebastian Veron have lots of the ball!

8 Join Arsenal!

9 Superglue Ole Gunnar Solskjaer to the subs bench!

10 Play them in the League Cup!

"You can... quote me on that"

"**Without being too harsh on David Beckham, he cost us the match.**"
Ian Wright refuses to totally blame David Beckham for England's defeat against Argentina in France '98.

"**I'm as happy as I can be – but I have been happier.**"
Ugo Ehiogu shows that no matter what, he's never fully satisfied!

"**Leeds is a great club and it's been my home for years, even though I live in Middlesbrough.**"
How does Leeds defender Jonathan Woodgate get home from training every day, then?

"**I can see the carrot at the end of the tunnel.**"
That's well weird from Stuart Pearce – most of us just see light at the end of ours!

"**I took a whack on my left ankle, but something told me it was my right.**"
Lee Hendrie – a man who truly doesn't know his left from right!

"**I was watching football on TV when it flashed up that my mate George Ndah had scored against Birmingham. My first reaction was to give him a ring, but then I remembered he was out there playing.**"
Ade Akinbiyi isn't the sharpest – and we're not talking about his shooting, either!

"**I'm going to sue Alan Hansen – he used to make me head all the balls. If I get Alzheimers in ten years, I'm taking civil action against him!**"
Mark Lawrenson on his ex-Liverpool team-mate Alan Hansen. That must be why Lawro talks so much rubbish!

DID YOU KNOW?

In 1990, Man. United tried to sign a youngster called Chaz Hodges, but Hodges turned them down coz the club said he needed a haircut!

SEE YOU JIMMY!

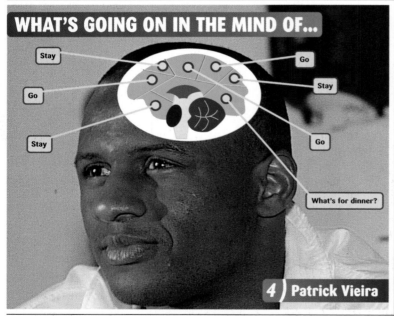

Chelsea striker Jimmy Floyd Hasselbaink is hiding somewhere in this crowd shot. But can you spot the cheeky Dutchman?

WHAT'S GOING ON IN THE MIND OF...

Stay

Go

Stay

Go

Stay

Go

What's for dinner?

4 | Patrick Vieira

IT COULD HAPPEN... *YEAH RIGHT!*

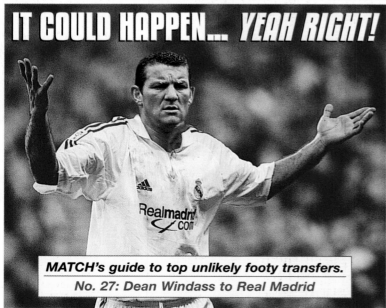

MATCH's guide to top unlikely footy transfers.
No. 27: Dean Windass to Real Madrid

BECKHAM

"Er, can I have a break please, Mr Sculptor?"

Nope, we can reveal that Becks ain't big-headed!

HIGH FIVE...

TOP FOOTY SLAPHEADS: Is it just coincidence that some of the world's best players are bald?

 1. ZINEDINE ZIDANE
 2. RONALDO
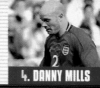 3. FABIEN BARTHEZ
 4. DANNY MILLS
 5. HASAN SAS

IN HEAD ROLE!

When do you know that yer famous? When Alistair McGowan does a rubbish impression of you on the telly? When you pick yer nose in public and the pictures make the cover of every newspaper? When you start going out with Jordan? Well, probably all those, but most of all it's when you have a waxwork made of you in Madame Tussauds.

Of course, nobody's more famous than David Beckham right now, which means the Manchester United star was always guaranteed to be immortalised in wax! Golden Balls was prepared in time for the summer's Goal exhibition at Madame Tussauds. The process was long and complicated – Becks had his face measured using calipers, then he had his eyeballs matched, and last of all a team of sculptors spent ages copying the England captain's features.

You can still get down there and check out the Becks model up close to see what all the fuss is about. But a message to any Man. City fans – please don't turn up with a box of matches and try to melt the thing, it's priceless!

"Oi MATCH, I've got all my eyes on you lot!"

RIO'S TABLE TENNIS SECRET!

He may have been one of the star performers at the 2002 World Cup, but Rio Ferdinand is not just top banana at footy. The Leeds centre-back is also the best table tennis player in the England team, and gave everyone a good hiding during the World Cup! Rio whupped ass during the summer and is looking for somebody to give him a challenge in the Premiership this season. But Rio's not the only footy star to excel in other sports! Here's our MATCH guide to the footy players who enjoy a break from the beautiful game!

A BRIEF HISTORY OF FOOTY STARS AND OTHER SPORTS!

1 The first footy stars who were champs in other sports were Denis and Leslie Compton of Arsenal in the '40s. The brothers both played footy for The Gunners and cricket for county teams, with Denis being one of England's big cricket stars of the time!

2 Paul Gascoigne got in a load of bother during the 1990 World Cup when he was caught playing tennis by manager Bobby Robson the night before a big game! The midfield star had been playing in the sun without his shirt on, and Robson went ballistic before Gazza ran off!

3 Callum Davidson of Leicester is an expert golfer – just like most footy players reckon they are! But Davidson has a handicap of scratch, which is not far off professional standards. Flash!

4 Way before playing for Man. United and not playing for his country at footy, Roy Keane used to be into boxing. But his preferred sport was Gaelic football, which toughened him up into the monster he is today!

5 Young Newcastle striker Tresor Lua Lua used to be a talented gymnast, but he gave it up to channel his energies into making big bucks in footy. That's how he can do his cool back-flip celebration!

>PLANET FOOTY!<

DID YOU KNOW?
Liverpool used to play in blue and white checked shirts, and Everton were the first team to play at Anfield!

TOP 5!
BIGGEST TRANSFERS ...EVER!

Feeling flush? Good – you'll need nuff dollar to sign these bad boys!

£48.0 million

1. ZINEDINE ZIDANE
Juventus to Real Madrid
Summer 2001

£37.5 million

2. LUIS FIGO
Barcelona to Real Madrid
Summer 2000

£35.4 million

3. HERNAN CRESPO
Parma to Lazio
Summer 2000

£32.6 million

4. GIANLUIGI BUFFON
Parma to Juventus
Summer 2001

£31.0 million

5. CHRISTIAN VIERI
Lazio to Inter Milan
Summer 1999

ROY KEANE IN TERMINATOR 2!

I'll be back - to stick it up your *@!!&*@*, Mick McCarthy!

FOOTY STARS IN THE MOVIES!

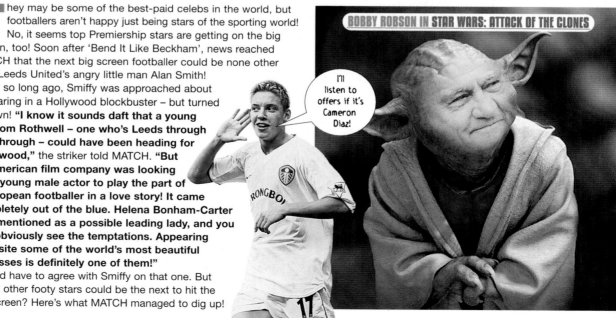

BOBBY ROBSON IN STAR WARS: ATTACK OF THE CLONES

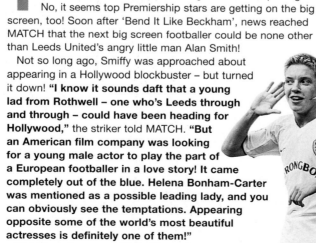

I'll listen to offers if it's Cameron Diaz!

They may be some of the best-paid celebs in the world, but footballers aren't happy just being stars of the sporting world! No, it seems top Premiership stars are getting on the big screen, too! Soon after 'Bend It Like Beckham', news reached MATCH that the next big screen footballer could be none other than Leeds United's angry little man Alan Smith!

Not so long ago, Smiffy was approached about appearing in a Hollywood blockbuster – but turned it down! **"I know it sounds daft that a young lad from Rothwell – one who's Leeds through and through – could have been heading for Hollywood,"** the striker told MATCH. **"But an American film company was looking for a young male actor to play the part of a European footballer in a love story! It came completely out of the blue. Helena Bonham-Carter was mentioned as a possible leading lady, and you can obviously see the temptations. Appearing opposite some of the world's most beautiful actresses is definitely one of them!"**

We'd have to agree with Smiffy on that one. But which other footy stars could be the next to hit the big screen? Here's what MATCH managed to dig up!

HIGH FIVE...

BEST BRAZIL PLAYERS EVER: It's a tough call, but see what you reckon to these Samba kings!

 1. PELE
 **2. SOCRATES**
 **3. RONALDO**
 4. RIVALDO
5. ZICO

MARTIN KEOWN IN PLANET OF THE APES!

DWIGHT YORKE IN AUSTIN POWERS

HARRY KEWELL IN HARRY POTTER

GIANFRANCO ZOLA IN LORD OF THE RINGS (AS FRODO)

Harry Potter AND THE SORCERER'S STONE

WAYNE BRIDGE IN WAYNE'S WORLD

PHIL THOMPSON IN PINOCCHIO

RU... POP OR FOOTY?

It never used to be like this, but now footy stars share the same celebrity status as pop stars. If it came to the crunch, though, would you be more Backstreet than Blackburn?

Westlife (A) V West Ham (B)

Posh (A) V Becks (B)

Eminem (A) V Everton (B)

So Solid Crew (A) V Crewe Alexandra (B)

Shaggy (A) V Darren Anderton (B)

Robbie Williams (A) V Robbie Fowler (B)

Kylie (A) V Dean Kiely (B)

Craig David (A) V Craig Bellamy (B)

Sum 41 (A) V Sunderland (B)

Fatboy Slim (A) V David Ginola (B)

Mostly A
You're a pop person, aincha? Put this down and get a copy of Smash Hits instead, you big footy fraud!

Mostly B
Nice one, you know yer fake manufactured music from yer top footy action! Gerrin!

THE UNOFFICIAL & NOT WHOLLY

Born in Chester in December 1979, Michael Owen has gone on to become European Footballer Of The

1 — At the age of six months, young Mikey was already a footy nut

Man on! Gaga! Back door!

2 — Signed up by Liverpool, he made his debut at the age of 11...

Yeah, two goals and no homework!

3 — It wasn't long before he was representing his country...

And what's your name, little boy?

7 — Back in England, Owen was a star...

Bling bling! This Rolex is worth more than you, mate!

8 — ...but of course, the goalposts had moved.

If I can just get these back in the right spot!

9 — Much more was expected of the youngster...

Blinkin' hell. Only five goals this game.

13 — Owen tried other sports...

Yikes!

14 — ...and other careers...

This only does Mach Three? My Jag's faster than that!

15 — ...but none of them really worked out.

Argh, me hamstring!

19 — He hit a double in the Cup final...

Wahey! Eat that, Arsenal!

20 — ...and secured the UEFA Cup for Liverpool!

Get in! Now for the Germans!

21 — Nobody could deal with Owen's pace again...

Have some of that!

HIGH FIVE...

MAN. UNITED'S WORST EVER SIGNINGS:
Red Devils' fans won't forget these five flops!

1. KAREL POBORSKY   2. JORDI CRUYFF   3. MARK BOSNICH   4. JUAN VERON   5. MASSIMO TAIBI

TRUE STORY OF MICHAEL OWEN!

Year 2001 and one of the world's biggest stars. Here's the story of how it all happened... well, sort of!

4

...against Argentina in the 1998 World Cup!
Wahey! Catch me if you can!

5

There, he scored one of the goals of the tournament...
You can't get near me, nah-nah-nah-nah-nah!

6

Out my way, ginge. I'm on my way to immortality!
...turning himself into a legend!

10

Hee-yah! Eat my frustration!
...forcing poor Owen to break people's legs.

11

Pressure and injuries were getting too much...
I... can't... do... it...

12

NORTHWICH VICTORIA F.C.
Get out and stay out, you donkey!
...and a loan move didn't work out.

16
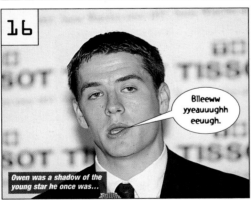
Blleeww yyeauuughh eeuugh.
Owen was a shadow of the young star he once was...

17

Who am I?
...and he really had to do some thinking.

18
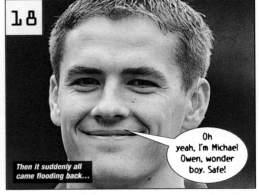
Oh yeah, I'm Michael Owen, wonder boy. Safe!
Then it suddenly all came flooding back...

22

Ha, ha! Maybe that'll shut Geoff Hurst up for a bit!
...and he netted a great hat-trick in Munich...

23

Zis is great. You owe me.
... and the European Footballer Of The Year award!

24

I'll take the armband now Becks - you'll be past it in 2006!
Owen didn't add the World Cup to his collection, but at 22, there's still time!

USELESS MATCH STAT!

Over the last nine seasons, Ronaldo scored 136 goals in 165 league games. That means he's got an 82 per cent chance of scoring!

CAN ENGLAND WIN EURO 2004?

5 reasons why we'll be lifting the trophy...

1 The experience gained at the 2002 World Cup was vital. Having learned from their mistakes and felt the full pressure of an international competition, the players will be well up for it in 2004!

2 Many of the England squad, like Becks, Nicky Butt, Sol Campbell and Paul Scholes will be at their peak, while youngsters like Michael Owen, Ashley Cole, and Steven Gerrard will be a couple of years wiser.

3 Hopefully, the FA can reduce the number of matches that everyone has to play, which will mean the squad won't be so tired before the tournament starts!

4 Victories against major powers like Argentina and Germany have proved that Sven's men can take on any team in the world and give them a run for their money.

5 Sven's only just started his job with England. His first task was to get us to the World Cup, but now his masterplan can really take off!

5 reasons why we'll get bombed again...

1 England still haven't mastered the passing possession play that's so vital in international footy. With the style of English football, and the lack of English players who can pass the ball around, they'll suffer the same fate.

2 No matter how good England are, France, Italy, Holland, Spain, Sweden, Portugal and Germany are all pretty tasty themselves!

3 The humidity over in Portugal will again be too much for the players, and with little chance of reducing the number of domestic games, the players will be too tired to perform at their best.

4 Expectation and hype will again outweigh realistic chances. Despite our players' talents, they don't match up to the skill levels of many other countries.

5 Sven's tactics are one-dimensional and built around a counter-attacking Italian style. While we stick to this ploy, we will always be beaten at some point!

CONCLUSION

WE CAN WIN IT, BUT NEED TO LEARN FROM OUR MISTAKES!

FOOTBALL'S TOP TEN HORROR

10 Louis Saha Fulham

Saha's blonde dreadlocks may have been pretty cool, but when the Fulham striker emerged from the dressing room one day with a spiky punk version, it shook the footy world to its foundations. Did he not brush it after getting out of bed? Did he tire of braiding it? Only Saha knows the answer to that one!

I'VE GOT A BLIND BARBER RATING 54%

9 Juan Pablo Sorin Cruzeiro

Argentina wing-back Sorin chose the greatest sporting event on earth to prove once and for all that Argentinians are the worst for hair tomfoolery in world footy! Along with team-mates Mauricio Pochettino and Diego Placente, Sorin completed a defensive trio of horror hair! His curly, armpit-length barnet bares all the hallmarks of someone without the vaguest idea about style. Poor lad!

I'VE GOT A BLIND BARBER RATING 59%

7 Ronaldinho Paris Saint Germain

The horror that England fans felt when Ronaldinho chipped David Seaman at the World Cup was only second to the horror they felt at looking at the permed Brazil striker. Nobody will ever work out why Ronaldinho decided to suddenly swap a respectable number one all over for a Michael Jackson 1984 scarecut, but one thing's for certain – it just don't suit him, Jacko or anyone else!

I'VE GOT A BLIND BARBER RATING 64%

6 Lorenzo Amoruso Rangers

Rangers defender Amoruso keeps his hair slicked back on his head using one simple method – by not washing it! Well, that might not be strictly true, as it's actually a complete MATCH guess – but by the looks of things, he could do with some of the shampoo David Ginola famously uses – and sharpish mate!

I'VE GOT A BLIND BARBER RATING 68%

4 Rory Delap Southampton

Before getting a close crop on joining Southampton, Delap sported a haircut that's commonly known as the 'greasebowl'. Perhaps he'd been watching too much Italian footy and tried to grow the traditional Italian grease locks, but it didn't work. Obviously someone had a word with Rory, coz his new crop is much better now, but memories of that medium-length disaster linger on!

I'VE GOT A BLIND BARBER RATING 78%

3 Umit Davala Inter Milan

David Beckham's biggest contribution to the 2002 World Cup wasn't the great penalty against Argentina – it was the idea that mohican haircuts are socially acceptable. On Becks, any haircut looks good – on everyone else it doesn't. So when Clint Mathis and Christian Ziege wheeled out mohawks in Japan, it was all wrong. But king of the skanky mohican was Turkey's Umit Davala.

I'VE GOT A BLIND BARBER RATING 83%

HIGH FIVE...

FACIAL HAIR DISASTERS: Face fuzz is always a bit hit and miss, but these are definitely miss!

1. GARRY BIRTLES   2. ALEXEI LALAS   3. BATISTUTA   4. SHAUN TEALE   5. OLOF MELLBERG

HAIRCUTS!

Hairdo? Hairdon't more like, if this selection of bloomin' awful barnets is anything to go by!

With the amount of money footballers make, you'd think they would know the telephone number of a half-decent hairdresser. After all, how wrong can you go, getting yer unruly locks trimmed? Unfortunately, it seems most of yer top footy stars can go wrong – very wrong indeed!

8   Paul Warhurst   Bolton

Bolton Wanderers has always been a club where men are men, ever since Nat Lofthouse knocked people in the back of the net in the 1950s. So why a big, strong lad like Paul Warhurst feels the need to play wearing an Alice band is beyond MATCH. His long locks may be acceptable down south in that fancy London, where men are all shandy-drinking wusses, but in Bolton it's a no-no!

I'VE GOT A BLIND BARBER RATING 62%

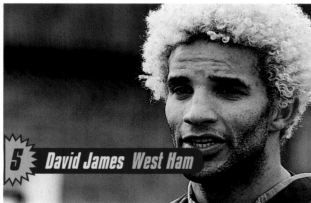

5   David James   West Ham

David James is a top mate of MATCH, but now and again, we have to have a word. His pre-World Cup strategy to try and force his way into Sven Goran Eriksson's first XI by disguising himself as a sheep definitely wasn't a top plan. Fortunately, this bush went pretty quickly and Jamo did go to the World Cup!

I'VE GOT A BLIND BARBER RATING 71%

2   Robbie Savage   Birmingham City

Robbie's blonde locks have become the envy of every football fan across the country. That's why he's constantly abused by supporters at every away ground – the opposition fans are jealous of his flash mane. So if they tell you they actually think it makes him look like a girl, and that he's just a flash nancy with more money than style, it's just because they're jealous. Er, probably!

I'VE GOT A BLIND BARBER RATING 89%

> Now I have the money to get all me hair cut off, like!

1   Ronaldo   Inter Milan

The Brazil striker wheeled out this freak cut during the 2002 World Cup. Some people wondered if he'd had another emotional breakdown like in 1998, but it turned out the Inter Milan man was just trying to cheer everyone up! **"I didn't do it to copy David Beckham,"** he claimed afterwards. **"I did it for a joke."** And what a joke it was! Sadly for Ronaldo, though, the laugh was on him!

I'VE GOT A BLIND BARBER RATING 93%

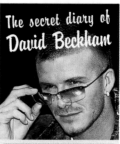

PREMIERSHIP S

MICHAEL
OWEN
PAGE 16

RUUD
VAN NISTELROOY
PAGE 34

THIERRY
HENRY

UPER STRIKERS!

Want to know how to make it as a striker? Read how the best of the best did it then!

L et's face it, every player wants to be a striker. He's the guy who grabs all the glory, and the fans always idolise goalscorers. But while it's great once you're there, it's not easy to reach those heady heights. To prove it, MATCH has targeted four of the world's deadliest marksmen to see how they made it to the highest level. They've got four very different stories too!

First up is **Michael Owen**, England's boy wonder, who's made it by finding one club and sticking with them until he made the big time. That's nothing like Man. United's **Ruud van Nistelrooy** – our second striker – who had to fight his way from club to club before making his mark in the Premiership.

Meanwhile, the ever-crafty **Thierry Henry** rocketed from the back streets of Paris to World Cup and Euro glory and **Jimmy Floyd Hasselbaink** had to find a club outside his native Holland to get his big-time break.

They may have got to the top by different routes, but these guys still have one thing in common – all of 'em are Super Strikers and MATCH tells their amazing stories here!

JIMMY FLOYD HASSELBAINK

PAGE 50

PAGE 76

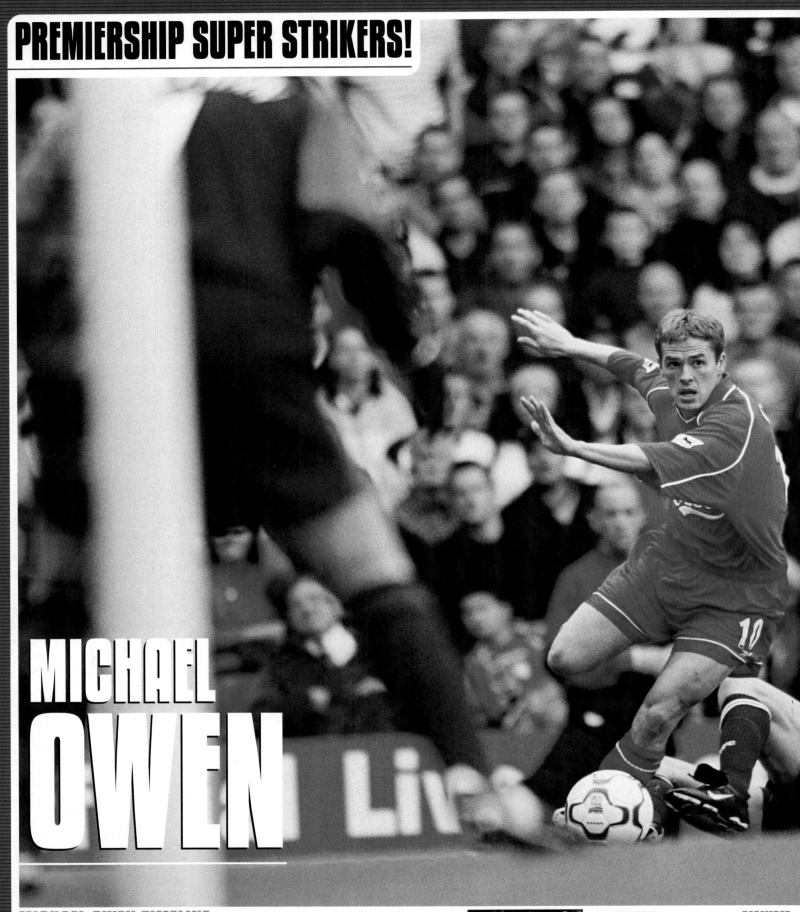

PREMIERSHIP SUPER STRIKERS!

MICHAEL OWEN

MICHAEL OWEN TIMELINE...

PRIMARY SCHOOL PRODIGY
First signs of a football legend after becoming the youngest player for Deeside Primary School in North Wales.

1992

WRECKS RUSH'S RECORD
Beats the schoolboy scoring record of Liverpool goal legend Ian Rush.

SEPTEMBER
LIVERPOOL LAD
Despite being an Everton fan, starts playing at the Liverpool Centre Of Excellence.

1993

LILLESHALL LAD
Selected as one of 16 young stars to go to the FA's Lilleshall Centre Of Excellence.

1994

SCHOOLBOY STAR
Starts scoring for England schoolboys, notching on his debut for the under-15s and under-18s.

1995

DECEMBER
THE PROFESSIONAL
Signs pro forms with Liverpool on 17th birthday, despite interest from Manchester United.

1996

MAY
PREMIERSHIP DEBUT
Scores on his debut for Liverpool, at Selhurst Park against Wimbledon.

DECEMBER
UNDER-21 JOY
At just 18, Michael finds the net on his debut for the under-21s against Greece.

1997

> **"He scored adult goals in schoolboy football, the sort of goals that would not have looked out of place in the Premiership. That's a sign of a rare talent."**
> John Owens, Michael's youth coach, spotted the striker's talent early on.

MATCH charts how Liverpool's striking star has set the footy world alight!

Michael Owen's become a goalscoring legend at Liverpool. Up there with the likes of Robbie Fowler, Ian Rush and Roger Hunt, his golden touch in front of goal has made him an icon at Anfield and one of the best strikers in the club's history.

Michael was always destined for greatness. After smashing Rush's goalscoring record at his primary school, and then joining The Reds' Centre Of Excellence, there was no stopping his progress. Two years at the FA's Lilleshall school honed his skills, and after scoring on his debut for the England under-15 and under-18 sides, Owen signed professional forms with Liverpool Football Club on his 17th birthday. He's never looked back, and has gone on to become a super striker.

Michael's rise from the little lad in Chester to become Liverpool and England's most dangerous goalscorer has been nothing short of incredible. Here, MATCH charts the crucial stages in his already fantastic footy career and reveals how he made it to the big-time!

CAREER FACTFILE
Born: December 14, 1979 in Chester
Nationality: English
Position: Striker
Height: 5ft 8ins
Weight: 10st 13lbs
Former clubs: None
Signed: From trainee
Liverpool debut: v Wimbledon, May 6, 1997
Total Liverpool games/goals: 205/111 (May 1997 to July 2002)
Trophies won at Liverpool: League Cup 2001, FA Cup 2001, UEFA Cup 2001, European Super Cup 2001.
International caps/goals: England 41/18 (February 1998 to September 2002)

FEBRUARY
FULL ENGLAND DEBUT
Becomes the youngest England player of the 20th century, aged 18 years and 59 days, against Chile at Wembley.

APRIL
YOUNG PLAYER AWARD
Named the PFA Young Player Of The Year by fellow pros.

MAY
DEBUT ENGLAND GOAL
Scores first senior goal for England against Morocco.

JUNE
WORLD CUP STAR
Nets a wonder goal against Argentina in France 98.

1998

MAY
TOP RED
Finishes the 1998-99 season as The Reds' top scorer with 18 Premiership goals.

1999

JANUARY
HAMSTRING WORRY
Receives intensive treatment on hamstring injuries which have interrupted his season.

JUNE
EURO OUT
Scores against Romania at Euro 2000 but England crash out in the group stages.

2000

MAY
HONOURS GALORE
Scores two late goals to win the FA Cup against Arsenal, adding to his League Cup and UEFA Cup winners' medals.

SEPTEMBER
MUNICH HAT-TRICK
England thrash Germany 5-1 in World Cup qualifier and Owen nets a stunning hat-trick.

2001

DECEMBER
TOP EURO AWARD
Named European Footballer Of The Year by top Euro footy journalists.

2002

APRIL
ENGLAND CAPTAIN
Captains England for the first time in the 4-0 win over Paraguay at Anfield.

JUNE
WORLD CUP SCORER
Scores against Denmark in the 2002 World Cup, also netting against Brazil in the quarter-finals.

1995

SCHOOLBOY STAR FOR LIVERPOOL & ENGLAND

Already a shining star in Liverpool's School Of Excellence, Michael Owen's name was on the lips of all the club's coaching staff. His speed, touch, ability and instinct for goal was, even in his early teens, not like anything seen since the days of Robbie Fowler.

For Liverpool he was moving through the youth ranks nicely, progressing at each level. Although he was small in size, he had no problem mixing it with the bigger defenders. On the international stage, he was already looking a natural too. Michael scored an incredible 12 goals in just seven games for England schoolboys. Liverpool's secret was now out – they had one very special talent on their hands who could take the world by storm.

1997

GOAL-DEN DEBUT

Michael had already got a taste of the action at both youth and reserve-team level for Liverpool, but manager Roy Evans had decided it was time to give him his first-team debut. Involved in a squad which included big names like Jamie Redknapp, John Barnes and Steve McManaman, Owen's special day came on May 6, 1997 when he made his debut as a 57th minute sub in a Premiership game against Wimbledon at Selhurst Park.

The livewire striker soon settled into the game and began causing problems for the shell-shocked Wimbledon defence. His pace and tricky skills on the ball, even at that early stage in his career, were clear to see.

In the 74th minute, Owen scored his first professional goal after slotting the ball home from just outside the penalty area and past goalkeeper Neil Sullivan. Fans in the 20,194 crowd had witnessed what would become a very regular sight in years to come – Michael Owen hitting the back of the opposition net.

1998

FEBRUARY RECORD BREAKER

Michael's breathtaking club form for Liverpool convinced England manager Glenn Hoddle to call him into the senior squad. The opponents were Chile on February 11 in a friendly game at Wembley. And when Owen pulled on the shirt that cold night, he became the youngest player to play for England in the 20th century – aged just 18 years and 59 days.

The speedy striker put on a dazzling display, and despite not getting on the scoresheet in the 2-0 defeat, he was awarded the Man Of The Match prize.

He didn't have to wait long for his first international goal, scoring on his third appearance against Morocco on May 27. That goal was a landmark, as it made him the youngest ever player to score for England.

1998

APRIL PFA YOUNG PLAYER

To cap a fine first full season in professional football, Michael was awarded the prestigious PFA Young Footballer Of The Year award in April 1998.

The award, as voted by his fellow professionals in England, came as the 18-year-old notched a quite amazing 23 goals in the 1997-98 season – 18 of which were scored in the Premiership.

It was also a season of scoring on debuts for the young striker. Owen netted on his first outing in the UEFA Cup against Celtic, in his League Cup bow against Grimsby and on his England Under-21 debut against Greece in December.

1998

JUNE WORLD CUP STAR

If one goal made the world sit up and take notice of Michael Owen, it was his fantastic solo effort against Argentina at the 1998 World Cup in France. Having been named in Glenn Hoddle's 22-man squad for the event, he played in all three group games and scored against Romania.

But it was England's second round clash with mighty Argentina when the Liverpool lad scored one of the best World Cup goals in memory. After collecting the ball in the centre circle from David Beckham, Owen raced past two defenders before slotting the ball home high into the net past 'keeper Carlos Roa.

It was an outstanding goal, and although England lost to Argentina on penalties, the strike made Owen a superstar overnight.

1999

CHART-TOPPING SUCCESS

The prolific youngster had topped the scoring charts at Anfield in the 1998-99 season. He finished with 18 goals in the Premiership, including four in one game against Nottingham Forest, two in the FA Cup, two in the UEFA Cup and one in the Worthington Cup! Michael was looking every bit the world-class talent he had threatened to be – but bizarrely, he still attracted his fair share of critics that season.

He went six games without finding the net – a dry spell of epic proportions, according to the Press – but he back with those four goals against Forest. Sadly, his season ended early, after suffering hamstring trouble against Leeds on April 12. Owen didn't play again in that campaign and the problem would go on to trouble him throughout the next year. Would he bounce back?

2000

EURO 2000 JOY AND PAIN

Michael's dodgy hamstrings were the subject of much talk in the season leading up to the Euro 2000 championships. He returned to full-time training in August 1999 – and played a total of 27 games in the Premiership, scoring 11 goals – but Gerard Houllier wanted to protect him, so he was often substituted or rested.

As part of England's Euro 2000 squad, Owen started all three games against Portugal, Germany and Romania alongside Alan Shearer. He scored against Romania, but England weren't playing well and returned home after the group stage, so an international tournament again proved to be an unhappy experience for Owen.

2001

MAY TRIPLE JUMP

Man. United may have walked away with the Premiership again in 2000-01, but Liverpool were arguably the team of the season.

The first of the club's three trophies came in February after winning the Worthington Cup final against Birmingham City at the Millennium Stadium – where Owen was rested on the bench.

But he was back for the FA Cup final against Arsenal, and his two brilliant late goals allowed Liverpool to come from behind to win the famous cup. Next up was the UEFA Cup final against Alaves in May. He didn't score that night, but he did win a penalty as The Reds won 5-4 in a Golden Goal thriller. This time it was a season of triumph for both Owen and his club.

"Michael Owen has made as big an impact on world football as Cruyff, Maradona and Pele."
Owen's former England manager Kevin Keegan explains the impact of the Liverpool and England star.

2001

DECEMBER EUROPEAN AWARD

The Liverpool ace received one of the highest awards in European football when he was named European Footballer Of The Year. And Michael deserved it after scoring for his club and country all year.

His personal highlight was blasting a hat-trick past Germany in England's 5-1 rout in Munich. That put him way ahead in the voting, with Real Madrid striker Raul in second place and Bayern Munich 'keeper Oliver Kahn in third. He was presented with the award at Derby, where guess what? He scored in a 1-0 Liverpool win!

2002

WORLD CUP HEARTACHE

England's most reliable source of goals played in his second World Cup finals in Japan. He looked sharp after worries about a groin problem, but didn't score in the group games against Sweden, Argentina or Nigeria, though he did win a penalty against old foes Argentina and hit the post in the historic 1-0 win over the highly-rated South Americans.

England faced Denmark in round two and Owen definitely had his shooting boots on, scoring the second with a poacher's goal in an emphatic 3-0 win.

Now, in the biggest game of his life, he faced the challenge of gunning down Brazil in the quarter-finals. He opened the scoring in the 23rd minute after latching on to a defensive error, but in the end Brazil were too classy and won 2-1. England went home, but Owen had again showed he could score goals on the world's biggest stage.

>PLANET FOOTY!<

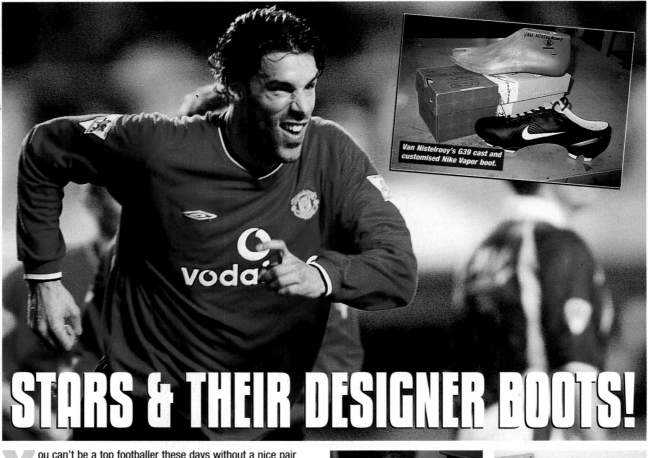

Van Nistelrooy's G39 cast and customised Nike Vapor boot.

STARS & THEIR DESIGNER BOOTS!

You can't be a top footballer these days without a nice pair of customised boots. Whatever the brand, whoever the star, they'll make sure they get their boots made to fit perfectly. MATCH went to Montebelluna in Italy to visit the fascinating Nike boot factory – and here's a little secret. While the security guards weren't watching, we sneaked into the special room for customised boots!

We found boots for everyone – Ronaldo (Inter Milan), Ruud van Nistelrooy (Man. United), Thierry Henry and Sylvain Wiltord (Arsenal), Marcelo Salas (Juventus), Jan Koller (Borussia Dortmund) and Neil Lennon (Celtic)! Each player has casts of their feet made, so their footy boots can be personalised and crafted to designer perfection.

From Ruud van Nistelrooy and his Vapors to the giant Czech striker Jan Koller and his enormous size 14 Air Zoom Total 90s, every boot is crafted for each individual player in the Italian factory. But that's not all! Each player has their own inner padding, studs and air pockets designed to fit their feet perfectly, so they can't possibly have a thing to moan about! Well, except for the French players, maybe!

Check out Jan Koller's massive size 14ers!

That Henry fella's got big feet!

"It's Marcelo Salas – bung me 20 new pairs in the post, will ya?"

DON'T BE SO RUUD!

Buuuurrp!

Man. United's flying Dutchman Ruud Van Nistelrooy is the king of bad manners! Welcome to his masterclass in anti-social antics!
This time: Belching while at the races with the Queen!

HE'S NOT ADE'S BEST!

MATCH reveals the final resting place of some of Ade Akinbiyi's 'goalbound' efforts!

No. 37) The south China sea

MATCH

PATRICK VIEIRA France

WORLD CUP

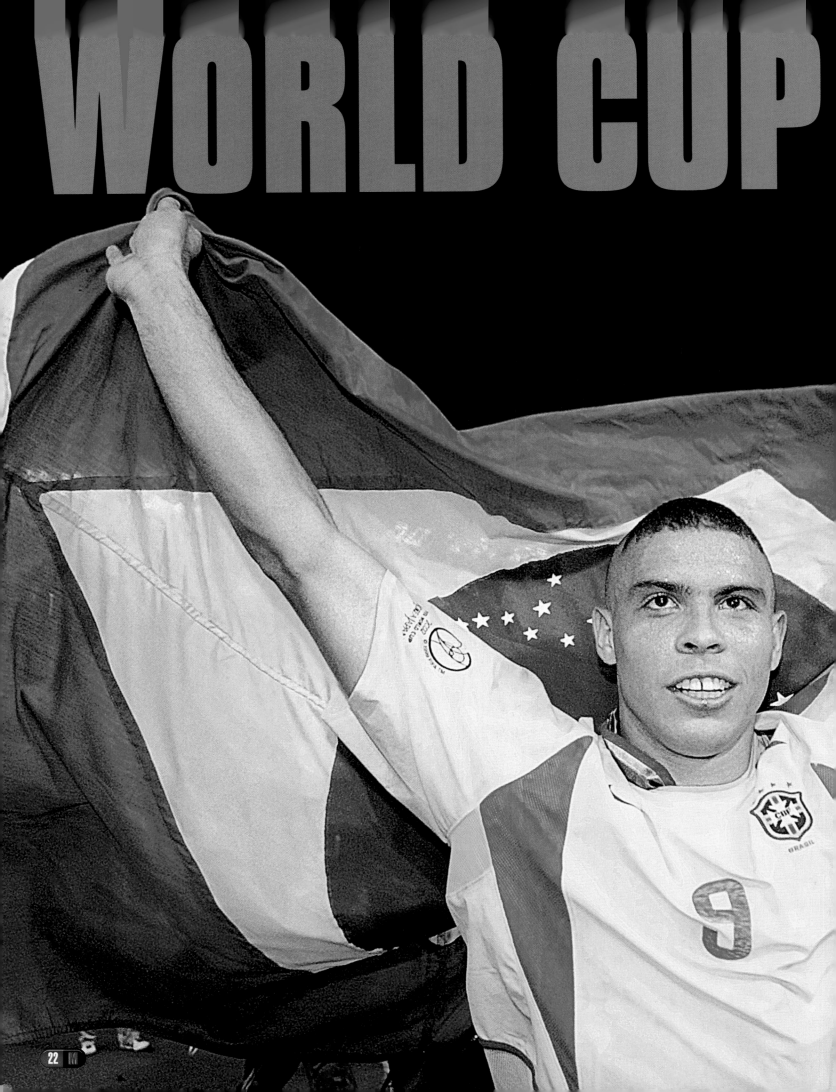

2002

DIARY OF A TOURNAMENT

THE AGONY...

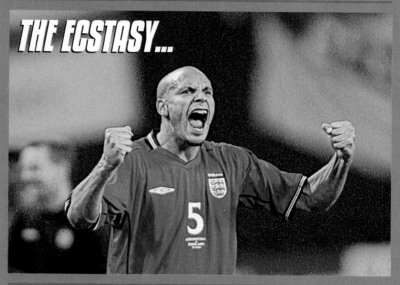

THE ECSTASY...

...& THE BIZARRE!

Senegal dance for joy after Bouba Diop puts them ahead!

Apparently, David was Trez annoyed!

SENEGAL SURPRISE HOLDERS FRANCE!

THE 2002 WORLD CUP WAS ONLY HALF AN HOUR OLD when we witnessed the first big shock of the tournament. Rank African outsiders Senegal, whose squad was almost entirely based in France, took on the holders in the Seoul Stadium and handed out a massive upset.

Just 30 minutes in, France were rocked by Senegal's goal. The pacy striker El Hadji Diouf, heading for a move to Liverpool, did all the running by taking on and beating Frank Leboeuf before crossing into the penalty area. Emmanuel Petit's interception was an ugly mess as he pushed the ball against goalkeeper Fabien Barthez, and Pape Bouba Diop was lurking inside the six yard box to sweep home the rebound and stun the champions!

France tried to reply, but the Senegalese had shaken them up, and when Thierry Henry's shot hit the post and David Trezeguet was foiled by goalkeeper Tony Sylva, the game was up. France, the 1998 World Cup winners and victors at Euro 2000, had been beaten by a team full of unknowns, playing in their first World Cup finals. It was a stunning result, but French coach Roger Lemerre still remained confident about his team's World Cup hopes after the game. A little bit too confident, perhaps.

"Am I disappointed by this?" he responded to post-match questioning. "Not really. We don't have to panic. We have two more matches left. France will go to the second round and at present anything is possible." It all sounded too easy according to Lemerre, but it didn't actually work out that way. France had left themselves a mountain to climb and the rest of the teams in the tournament took note – the holders were vulnerable. If they could lose so early on, anything was possible. As for Senegal, they milked the moment, and rightly so.

"This result is the biggest moment for our team and this World Cup," said coach Bruno Metsu. "We're delighted to have caused such an upset. We were lucky at times during the game but then so were France."

May 31 The Big Kick-Off

After weeks, months and even years of waiting, the tournament finally gets under way with the usual mad opening ceremony, and despite the threat of rain, the crowds pack into the stadium to see the action. In fact, 15,000 people turn up three hours before kick-off!

The main attraction, of course, is the first game of the 2002 tournament, when World and European Champions France take on World Cup rookies Senegal. The whole world sees it as a foregone conclusion, but the well-organised, talented Senegalese pull off the tournament's first big shock as they achieve an unlikely 1-0 win. Complacent France are rocked to their roots, but it's fantasy time for Senegal. **"We have realised our dreams and I am very satisfied,"** says Senegal coach Bruno Metsu after the game. **"It is the result of 18 months of hard work by the entire team. We are very happy with this incredible feat."**

June 1 Goals Galore

The first full day of the competition sees a supposedly understrength Germany shock everyone with an 8-0 win over sad Saudi Arabia. Denmark get off to a flyer as well, with two Jon Dahl Tomasson goals sinking Uruguay 2-1. It's hard to believe he's the same player who was so rubbish for Newcastle United just a few seasons earlier, but for Uruguay, it's all too true!

Liverpool fans delight at the news that Gerard Houllier has signed El Hadji Diouf, Senegal's hot frontman, but the big story of the day for the home teams is Ireland's opening game against Cameroon. Sunderland's Patrick Mboma puts the Africans ahead on 32 minutes, but Matt Holland is the hero as his low 52nd minute shot earns a 1-1 draw. **"It's a fantastic feeling to score,"** he says afterwards. **"And the draw is a good result for us, even if we did have the better chances."**

June 2-3 Group Of Death Gets Going

The first game on Sunday is Argentina's clash with Nigeria. They win 1-0 and are full of confidence. **"We are just going to get better and better every day,"** boasts Juan Sebastian Veron. England's fever pitch build-up is finally over, as they get their campaign going with a 1-1 draw against Sweden. In the day's other games, well-fancied Spain overcome Slovenia 3-1, while Paraguay and South Africa play out a 2-2 draw.

Monday sees Brazil and Italy both get going, and both secure three points. The Azzurri see off Ecuador 2-0 – with Vieri grabbing both goals – while Brazil's win is a little more controversial. They rely on a dodgy penalty decision to beat Turkey 2-1, and Rivaldo shocks the world with his play-acting. Turkey manager Senol Gunes is not pleased, to say the least. **"I'm not in a position to judge the referee. We controlled Brazil but we couldn't control the referee,"** is his take on events.

June 4-5 Hosts Home In

South Korea break an unwelcome duck by grabbing their first World Cup win, a 2-0 victory over a woeful Poland side. **"I am very, very happy,"** says manager Guus Hiddink in the post-match Press conference – hardly a surprise! Japan start slightly less impressively, as they draw 2-2 against Belgium, despite playing some good football – with Inamoto and Suzuki notching the goals.

June 5 sees the tournament's second big shock, as a talented Portugal side find themselves 3-0 down against the USA. Figo and co. manage to pull two goals back but can't do enough to salvage a point, and the

Super Sol soars over Sweden to put The Three Lions ahead!

Our Sven wasn't Swedish for this game!

At least England fans got their hands on one World Cup!

SWEDE & SOUR FOR SVEN

SVEN GORAN ERIKSSON MAY BE SWEDISH, BUT HE GOT NO favours from his fellow countrymen when England's World Cup opened against the Scandinavians in Saitama on June 2.

England's preparations were far from ideal in the build-up to the game, with several players battling for fitness. Nicky Butt and Kieron Dyer weren't considered ready to start the game, but captain David Beckham was, which gave England a major boost. Just over 20 minutes had gone when a corner from Becks was headed home by Sol Campbell, and England were off and running.

But the Swedes had other ideas, and took advantage of a lacklustre England in the second half. Beckham only lasted an hour, by which time Niclas Alexandersson had equalised.

A point wasn't exactly a disaster, but the performance gave cause for concern. **"All credit to Sweden,"** muttered captain Becks. **"They carried on going and kept on fighting, got the goal and then had a few chances. David Seaman kept us in the game, I thought. We felt we played some really good football in the first half, and we're pleasantly pleased, because we could have ended up losing the game."**

Rivaldo's thigh is actually right next to his nose, you know!

RIVALDO'S A CHEAT

HAVING JUST CONVERTED A LATE PENALTY TO give Brazil a narrow victory over Turkey in the opening game of Group C, Rivaldo showed his darker side with a disgraceful piece of play-acting.

The game was petering out when Turkey's Hakan Unsal stroppily blasted the ball at Rivaldo as he waited to take a corner. That wasn't good, but Rivaldo's behaviour was far worse – the ball struck him on the thigh but he threw himself to the turf, clutching at his face in pretend agony.

Unsal was sent-off, but despite protests, Rivaldo got away with a fine. And he wasn't even sorry.

"Obviously I exaggerated the incident for the guy to be sent off," he boasted. **"The ball hit my hand and my leg, not in the face, but that kind of attitude must not be allowed on the pitch. He deserved a red card."** Boo!

GERMANY'S DREAM 8

'NEVER UNDERESTIMATE THE GERMANS' IS ONE OF THE unofficial rules of world football, but surely no-one would have tipped Rudi Voller's team to go on such a goalscoring spree in their first game of the finals against Saudi Arabia.

The Saudis had no answer to Germany's ruthless aerial attacks, and succumbed to an embarrassing 8-0 defeat. It took Miroslav Klose just 20 minutes to get the ball rolling, and from then on, the goals flowed like water!

20 MINS: Ballack crosses for Klose to head home! **1-0!**
25 MINS: Ballack crosses and Klose heads home again! **2-0!**
40 MINS: Ziege crosses and Ballack heads home! **3-0!**
45 MINS: Frings crosses and Jancker heads home! **4-0!**
69 MINS: It's another header from Klose! **5-0!**
73 MINS: Ziege's corner and Linke's header! **6-0!**
84 MINS: Bierhoff pokes in from 20 yards! **7-0!**
90 MINS: Schneider's free-kick completes the job! **8-0!**

Klose was literally heading for the Golden Boot!

Becks seals the door on four years of hurt as Argentina are humbled!

Dave and Rio were quite exceptional!

CAPTAIN BECKS SETTLES HIS SCORE

IT WAS ONE OF THE MOST MAGICAL moments of the 2002 World Cup. England faced Argentina four years after the South Americans had eliminated them on penalties in the second round of the 1998 World Cup. So when the teams met again on June 7 in Group F, scores were there to be settled. Several England players were still outraged at the memory of how the Argentines gloated over their '98 win – and none more so than captain David Beckham, who was famously sent-off that day for clashing with rival midfielder Diego Simeone.

But this time it was England's turn to celebrate. A gritty performance resulted in a 1-0 win, with the vital goal scored by Beckham. Keeping his nerve despite deliberate distractions by Argentinian players, Beckham arrowed a 44th-minute penalty right down the middle of the goal. He celebrated like a man who had finally banished his demons, and the England team trotted off for their half-time break in great spirits. But could they hold on to their lead in the second half?

It certainly looked like it, as Eriksson's team played some top stuff in the second period. Owen, Beckham, Scholes and Sheringham all went close to adding to the single goal lead, but the final 20 minutes were as nervous as it gets, as Argentina piled on the pressure. Rio Ferdinand and Sol Campbell held firm though, allowing England to claim the win. Goalscorer and skipper Becks was dead chuffed afterwards.

"This feels better than it did four years ago," he grinned. **"It's unbelievable. It's been a long four years, it's been up and down, but this has topped it all off. It was terrifying taking the penalty because of their antics – the goalkeeper was telling me to put it one way, and Diego Simeone was trying to shake my hand, but that's just the way they play. We battled hard, did really well and got the result we needed!"**

whole of America celebrates – not! Germany look like they're going to secure another three points as they hold the Republic Of Ireland 1-0 until the 92nd minute, but they haven't reckoned on livewire Robbie Keane. His last-gasp equaliser sends the Irish into dreamland!

June 6-7 England's Finest Hour

Uruguay turn to violence as they dig into France and secure a dirty 0-0 draw. The match is notable for Thierry Henry's red card and subsequent suspension, as well as Dario Silva's potential leg-breaker that goes unpunished.

Group F continues with Sweden beating Nigeria 2-1 to send the Africans home, which means England really need a result when they play Argentina. England duly oblige though, and in one of the greatest moments of the nation's footy history, they smash Argentina 1-0 thanks to a David Beckham penalty. Wins for Cameroon and Spain, plus a 1-1 draw in Group A between Denmark and Senegal, complete the action of the week.

Off the pitch, Slovenia are plunged into drama when their star player Zlatko Zahovic is sent home. **"Zahovic continued with behaviour which is harmful to the atmosphere of the team,"** is the Slovenian Football Association's official explanation, but a strop over being left out of the side by the manager is the real reason.

June 8 Azzurri Fury

It's no surprise when troubled Slovenia go down 1-0 to South Africa, but the real talking points of the day concern two giants of the world game – Brazil and Italy. The Samba boys easily brush aside China 4-0 with an awesome display of attacking power, and look more and more impressive with every game they play. Not that China are that impressive, mind!

The Italy v Croatia game produces some fierce reactions. In the 55th minute, Christian Vieri's goal puts Italy 1-0 up, but the Italians sit back and eventually concede two quick Croatian goals. The Azzurri are spurred into action, and Vieri looks to have scored again but is controversially ruled offside. Then, Marco Materazzi's long ball into the box evades everyone and trickles home, but is also disallowed. **"We've been very unlucky,"** says Vieri afterwards. **"Everyone saw the game tonight, we shouldn't have lost it."**

June 9-10 Happy Japan

June 9 is all about Japan. Philippe Troussier's men take on a Russia team that hasn't shone yet, and they pull it out of the bag to secure their first ever World Cup win – Arsenal's forgotten man Junichi Inamoto scores the only goal of the game, his second of the tournament. The co-hosts are now in a strong position to qualify with four points from two games. Sunday also sees Mexico come from behind to beat Ecuador 2-1, while Turkey and Costa Rica play out a 1-1 draw.

Portugal go into their second game on June 10 knowing they must win, and this time everything goes to plan – they triumph 4-0, with Pauleta grabbing a World Cup hat-trick. Rui Costa finishes the scoring on 87 minutes to confirm that Portugal do actually mean business in the competition. The other co-hosts, South Korea, are in action again, and this time they draw 1-1 with USA, as do Tunisia and Belgium.

June 11 Irish Eyes Are Smiling

The first day of final group games sees a real shock. France – World and European Champions – are out, beaten by Denmark thanks to goals from Tomasson and

Keano grabs the goal that sends Ireland into raptures!

Happy? You could say that!

LAST-GASP ROBBIE DENIES GERMANY

BY THE TIME THE REPUBLIC OF IRELAND HAD TRAVELLED TO IBARAKI TO FACE GERMANY, the team was getting over the 'Keane factor' – the absence of inspirational captain Roy after a monumental sulk and strop session. Not only that, another Keane was, er, keen to make his mark in the tournament in his own style!

Striker Robbie did exactly that in Ireland's second game of the competition. Trailing to the Germans since Miroslav Klose's header on 23 minutes, the Irish toiled away for the rest of the match, busting a gut to break down a tough defence, marshalled superbly by goalkeeping great Oliver Kahn. It looked to be all for nothing until Keane pounced on a Niall Quinn flick-on to race into the box and slam a shot in off the post! Cue scenes of Irish fans going absolutely crazy!

"We felt like we would never score," said winger Kevin Kilbane. **"Damien Duff had a chance and then we had a few more opportunities after that. When Robbie scored it was one of the best feelings ever. Niall came on for us in the second half and changed the game around."**

Bullish Irish boss Mick McCarthy was unable to hide his joy at his side's comeback. **"I think we thoroughly deserved something out of it,"** he said. **"We battered the Germans and I think we gave them a good doing, to be honest. What's the point of coming home without a fight? It's just not going to happen!"**

THIERRY'S RED ALERT

FRANCE'S WORLD CUP CAMPAIGN LURCHED FROM ONE disaster to the next, with the second match against Uruguay – which was supposed to be their salvation – turning into a personal nightmare for star striker Thierry Henry.

The French, desperate for a victory to make up for the shock opening game defeat to Senegal, never recovered from the setback of seeing the Arsenal man sent-off after only 25 minutes. Tussling for possession, the striker lunged at Marcelo Romero with his studs raised and Mexican referee Ramos Rizo made the brave decision to send him off instantly. It was his first tackle, but it was high and late, and had to be punished.

Without Henry, the holders still went for it, but so did the South Americans in a flowing, end-to-end contest which had fans on the edge of their seats. A 0-0 draw meant both teams still had a chance of qualification going into the final group game, but neither actually made it into the second round.

Feeling sorry for them? Nope, thought not!

France – out!

Portugal – out!

THE LOSERS GO HOME

THERE WERE HUGE SHOCKS GALORE AS THE TOURNAMENT shaped up for the knockout stages, with minnows claiming prize scalps and big names tumbling all over the place.

Holders and pre-tournament favourites France bowed out with barely a whimper, losing 2-0 to Denmark and leaving South Korea & Japan without scoring a goal in their three matches. South American sensations Argentina – still complaining after losing 1-0 to England – went the same way after failing to beat Sweden, and another of the fancied nations, Portugal, also crashed out following a niggly defeat to the Koreans. Luis Figo's men lost to the USA, but had the chance to turn it around until a 1-0 defeat at the hands of the co-hosts cost them dearly.

African heavyweights Nigeria and Cameroon, tipped for a bright tournament, also failed to qualify for the second round, while Italy only just squeezed in thanks to Croatia's failure to beat an ordinary-looking Ecuador team. No-one was safe!

Nigeria – out!

Cameroon – out!

Michael Owen was his usual clinical self against Brazil!

"It's okay, it's going over... oops!" Seaman is beaten by Ronaldinho's lucky free-kick as England go out.

Rivaldo evades Sol Campbell's lunge to slot home Brazil's equaliser.

BRAZIL BURST ENGLAND'S BUBBLE

Ronaldinho sees red and has to go!

Big Dave gets big hugs. Aah!

Beating Denmark in the second round wasn't a problem, but coming up against Brazil in the quarter-finals was a different proposition. England had to pull something special out of the bag to beat the Samba superstars, who had become the tournament favourites.

England made a positive start, and one of the all-time legendary results seemed on when Michael Owen coolly put the Three Lions into the lead. But Brazil roared back, and after Rivaldo equalised on the verge of half-time, Ronaldinho's free-kick caught out 'keeper David Seaman to put the South Americans ahead. Despite Ronaldinho being dismissed shortly afterwards, England bowed out and Sven Goran Eriksson could only reflect on what might have been…

> **Where did it go wrong against Brazil, Sven?**
"It came down to two goals that came at very delicate moments of the match. They were killer moments. It's hard to respond after the first goal because it was just before half-time. Then you go out again and five minutes later, boom, there's another one. They tried, not in the best way, but I don't think you can expect that from a young team like ours. They will learn from this, though."

> **Any regrets from this World Cup?**
"You look at all the games you don't win, and wonder if things might have gone better if you had changed your line-up. You try to work out what the mistake was and then forget it, though. If you keep regretting what you do, you will go crazy sooner or later."

> **How was David Beckham's World Cup?**
"Beckham can play better football than he did in this tournament, but if you consider he had been away for seven weeks beforehand, I think he did very well. When you have those problems, you don't expect a player to be 100 per cent fit, as he was before Christmas."

> **Who really impressed you at the World Cup?**
"Nicky Butt, he was fantastic. He had come back from injury and hadn't been playing for a long time, but he played very, very well in all the games."

> **So how bright is England's future?**
"There are a lot of young players in the squad and they will get better by the time the European Championships come round. I had hoped to do better in the tournament but I think we've learned a lot about many things. I think we are the equal of any team in the world, and that's very good for a team as young as ours. English football is improving. It's getting better and better at club level and we will benefit from that."

Rommedahl. **"It is obvious we didn't deserve to progress to the second round,"** admits manager Roger Lemerre, **"but the French team will rebound."** In the other Group A decider, Senegal and Uruguay draw 3-3, and in a real rollercoaster of a game, Richard Morales misses a sitter that would've sent Uruguay through.

The other games see Germany qualify from Group E, and Ireland magnificently march on with a 3-0 win over Saudi Arabia – much to the delight and relief of Mick McCarthy. **"It's great,"** he says. **"Everybody has been telling us all week what a big game it is. You want to try sitting in the dugout, when your backside is on the bacon slicer. It's alright for everybody else, they can enjoy it. But the lads were brilliant."**

June 12 Argentina Exit

The only shock in Group B is that there are no shocks! Spain progress with maximum points, and they're joined by Paraguay, who beat hapless Slovenia 3-1. Spain's Joaquin can't hide his delight. **"I'm very happy. I think that maybe luck was on our side. We tried very hard and things worked out very well."**

The real action of the day comes in Group F, where Sven's men qualify thanks to a 0-0 draw with Nigeria, and Argentina become the latest superpower to be sent packing. They can't beat Sweden despite a lucky late equaliser, and for their supposed-to-be-good heroes, it's excuses time. **"If we made any mistakes, it was unwillingly,"** proclaims Gabriel Batistuta. **"The time is over and the pain is double. Sometimes the logic of football has no value at all."**

June 13 Big Boys Through

Italy look like they're going to suffer the same fate as France and Argentina, as they struggle to clinch the 1-1 draw they need to qualify. For long periods of the game, the Italians trail 1-0 to Mexico and on their way out, but a late Alessandro Del Piero goal saves them. **"There was a lot of pressure,"** explains manager Giovanni Trapattoni. **"I was happy to get a draw from a very hard game. It was a very important goal."** Both teams go through at the expense of Croatia and Ecuador.

The day's last round of games sees Brazil smash Costa Rica 5-2 to go through with maximum points, and they're joined by Turkey, who beat China 3-0. **"Brazil is getting stronger and better. If we continue playing like this, it is not difficult to imagine we will be in the final,"** says Rivaldo after the game. Scary!

June 14 Co-hosts Through

June 14 is D-Day for Portugal. With three points from two games, they need to win to be sure of qualifying, or draw and rely on other results. In the event though, other results don't come into it – Joao Pinto and Beto are sent off and Portugal are beaten 1-0 by South Korea. Yet again, a big football nation makes its sorry way home! Paulo Bento sums up the team by saying: **"The tree was twisted from the roots."** Whatever that means!

But it's jubilation all the way for South Korea – from never having won a World Cup game, they make it to the second round – which is the same story for Japan. Their 2-0 win over Tunisia is enough to send them into the next stage. The co-hosts are joined by Belgium and USA in the last 16, but still nobody in America seems to care about the World Cup!

June 15-18 Round Two Blues

Four out of the eight second round games see the favourites go through. England crush Denmark 3-0 to

The usually dependable Matt Holland hits the bar!

Spain go bonkers!

LUCK OF THE IRISH RUNS OUT!

MICK McCARTHY'S TOUGH REPUBLIC OF IRELAND SIDE BOWED OUT OF THE tournament with heads held high and pride intact, safe in the knowledge they'd given good value throughout the competition. Much is made of the so-called 'luck of the Irish', but when it came down to the second round clash with Spain, that mythical luck deserted the Republic in their hour of need.

Inspired by the dazzling Damien Duff – who took the opposition on at will – Ireland had pummelled the Spanish goal ever since Fernando Morientes put his team ahead after eight minutes. Ireland missed an Ian Harte penalty, but won another spot-kick in injury-time, which Robbie Keane converted in style.

The game went to extra-time and then penalties. Keane scored again, but Ireland's next three attempts – through Holland, Connolly and Kilbane – all missed and the Republic's fabulous adventure came to a heartbreaking end.

"I enjoyed myself," reflected Duff. **"It's been great playing against so many world-class players, and against Spain I think we bossed it. We've done brilliantly playing against the world's best."** McCarthy, who suffered a tough time over the Roy Keane saga, had the last laugh. **"I'm so proud to have had a chance to work with these players,"** he said. **"We'll leave with smiles on our faces and we've had a wonderful World Cup."**

Just one of many post-match celebrations from the Koreans!

★ PARK JI SUN

SOUTH KOREA SPARK FOOTBALL FEVER

FAR FROM JUST MAKING UP THE NUMBERS AT THE WORLD CUP, CO-HOSTS SOUTH KOREA excelled throughout the competition, thrilling their passionate supporters and impressing neutrals. The team, coached by former Holland manager Guus Hiddink, played some brilliant attacking football on its way to a surprise semi-final place, and claimed two major scalps along the way.

In the second round, the Koreans beat Italy 2-1. The game was an absolute classic, with the Italians stubbornly holding on to Christian Vieri's first-half goal until two minutes from the end, when Seol Ki-Hyeon equalised. In a frantic extra-time period, Francesco Totti was sent-off and the Italians had a goal disallowed before Ahn Jung-Hwan – who'd missed a penalty after only four minutes – struck a Golden Goal winner to spark crazy scenes of celebration.

Into the last eight, South Korea took on Spain. They weren't given a hope of winning, except by their own fans, but the Koreans won again – this time after a nerve-shredding penalty shoot-out. Spain were denied two good goals in Golden Goal time, again by controversial decisions, which allowed Hong Myung-Bo to strike the winning penalty. **"I cannot describe how I'm feeling,"** gushed Hiddink. **"I'm so happy for the boys. I think more dreams have come true now."**

And so they had. Those dreams were ended by Germany in the semi-finals, but no matter. The South Korean side, which finally finished fourth behind Turkey, were responsible for some of the tournament's most memorable images, and Asian footy was put firmly on the map at last.

Super Ronny pokes home the winner against Turkey!

CLASS WINS THE DAY IN SEMI-FINALS

South Korea came so close, but Germany were just too strong for them.

THE WORLD CUP SEMI-FINALS WERE A STRANGE MIX of teams. On the one hand, Germany and Brazil, two of international football's biggest players, survived the spate of giant-killing acts to make it through to the last four. But joining them were Turkey, who got better and better as the tournament progressed, and South Korea, the exciting co-hosts of the competition.

Germany and South Korea were the first to meet, in Seoul. As with most of Germany's matches in the World Cup, this was a tight affair. With Korean tails up, the Europeans didn't have an easy ride. Goalkeeper Oliver Kahn had to make an excellent early save before the Germans gradually got a grip of the game and scored the decisive goal on 75 minutes through Michael Ballack. But the inspirational midfielder had already been booked for a foul on the edge of his own penalty area as he denied Korea a clear goalscoring opportunity, and the yellow card meant he would miss the final through suspension anyway. "He still committed that tactical foul, which was utterly necessary," insisted German coach Rudi Voller after the game. **"He placed himself at the service not only of the team, but the whole of Germany – the entire country will understand him and applaud him for that."**

In the other semi-final, played the next day, favourites Brazil faced Turkey, who they had already beaten in the group stages. Again, it was a close one and tricky Turkey threatened on several occasions – not least when Alpay almost scored with a header. But Brazil edged it with a single goal – a fine individual strike from Ronaldo – who had grown in stature with every match he played in the Far East. His 49th-minute effort, toe-poked past Recber following a darting run past several Turkey defenders, was superb.

"We are very happy about winning this game but we haven't won the World Cup yet," warned Ronaldo. **"We shouldn't be too excited about it with the final still to come."**

So, Brazil v Germany. A classic awaited!

Ballack celebrates, even though he knows he'll miss the final!

boost confidence, Germany beat Paraguay 1-0 in the most boring game of the tournament so far, Brazil knock out Belgium, and Spain send Mick McCarthy's brave Ireland home after a cruel penalty shoot-out.

The other four games, however, are huge talking points. First, the USA beat Mexico to reach the quarters for the first time since 1930 – and only the second time in their history – then Turkey silence Japan by beating them 1-0. Senegal send Sweden home through Henri Camara's Golden Goal, after Anders Svensson had hit the post, but the biggest shock is supplied by South Korea, who amazingly beat Italy. Yet again the game is marred by dodgy refereeing, and again Italy are the victims as a perfectly good Golden Goal is ruled out. **"If one team should have advanced, it was Italy,"** says manager Giovanni Trapattoni, and it's hard to disagree.

June 19-22 Quarter Crunch!

England face Brazil in the first quarter-final, and despite Michael Owen striking first, two goals either side of half time are enough to send Brazil through to the semis. Germany and USA are next up, and yet again Germany pull off a 1-0 win. There's more World Cup controversy as the referee misses a goal-line handball from Torsten Frings which prevents an American goal.

Turkey beat Senegal with a Golden Goal from Ilhan Mansiz, but the biggest story comes when South Korea take on Spain. As the refereeing debate rumbles on, yet more ridiculous decisions see Spain expelled. First, Ivan Helguera's perfectly good header is ruled out for offside, then Morientes has a header disallowed because the ball apparently went out of play before it was crossed in; though TV replays show it was nowhere near. **"This is the quarter-finals of a World Cup, not a friendly played anywhere. Two goals disallowed – that has never been seen,"** fumes Morientes afterwards.

June 23-29 And Then There Were Two

Germany and South Korea line up for the first semi-final, and the game revolves around one man – Michael Ballack. The creative midfielder is booked in the second half, meaning he would miss the final if Germany got there, but he then goes on to score the only goal of the game. **"The entire country will understand him and applaud him,"** says manager Rudi Voller as the team celebrate a seventh World Cup final appearance.

It's down to Brazil and Turkey to see who'll join them, and the game goes as expected. Ronaldo scores the only goal – a brilliant effort soon after half-time – and Brazil go marching on. **"The goal was a toe-poke but it was an important goal,"** explains Ronaldo, the man of the moment. **"We are very happy about today's match, but we haven't won the title yet."**

June 30 Final Showdown

Brazil and Germany – two of the world's biggest names – meet for the final. Amazingly though, they've never played each other in the World Cup before, so there's no form to look at, and no history to spur on the teams. Not that they need it – this is the World Cup final here!

Germany start brightly but fail to score. In the second half, Oliver Kahn spills Rivaldo's shot and Ronaldo is onto it like a flash to put Brazil 1-0 up. Germany keep at Brazil, but when Ronaldo makes it 2-0, it's game over. **"I feel happiness and joy, probably the same joy the people of Brazil are feeling,"** says victorious coach Luiz Felipe Scolari. In a fantastic team effort, Ronaldo stands out with his eight goals, making him the World Cup's top scorer and MATCH's man of the tournament.

Ronaldinho proves there's more than just one super Ron!

Kahn can only watch as Ronaldo ruins German dreams!

RONALDO CROWNS BRAZIL CHAMPS!

BRAZIL AND GERMANY FACED EACH OTHER IN THE 2002 World Cup final in Japan's Yokohama Stadium, on June 30, with an amazing statistic doing the rounds. Since the introduction of the famous tournament, only two finals had ever been played *without* either of these nations being in it! Even more surprising was the fact that they'd never previously come up against each other in any match, at any stage, of any World Cup.

Brazil were obvious favourites to win a record-busting fifth world title, but Germany started positively as the South Americans took time to settle. Brazil came back into the game though, with Ronaldo missing two good chances and Kleberson hitting the post on the stroke of half-time as Brazil searched for the crucial opening goal.

From the restart, Germany twice went close themselves, especially when Oliver Neuville's blasted free-kick was tipped on to the post by Marcos. But Ronaldo wasn't to be denied. When Kahn – later to be named Player Of The Tournament – didn't hold Rivaldo's low strike, the Inter Milan forward buried the rebound.

Minutes later, the awesome number nine sealed the game, stroking home a fine finish to make it 2-0.

There was a certain amount of poetic justice for Ronaldo. In 1998 he had infamously suffered a fit on the eve of the final against France and struggled through the game. This was his moment, and he deserved it.

"I want to thank every member of our squad," he said. **"I fought for two years to overcome my injury, and I am very glad to have scored both the goals and help bring the fifth World Cup back to Brazil. I want to thank my family for all their support."**

But for 'keeper Kahn, who had been an outstanding performer in the previous matches, there was only bitter disappointment at losing the final, and he blamed himself for Brazil's opening goal. **"It's really frustrating when you make your one mistake of the tournament and get punished like that,"** he said, shaking his head. **"Nothing can console me after that, but life goes on."**

Indeed it does, but it won't be the same with another World Cup over. Roll on the next one – Germany in 2006!

No-one deserves it more than Ronaldo, the world's best player!

Gary Lineker was a Golden Boot winner – but when?

first XI

The 2002 World Cup was a real cracker, but how much do you know about previous competitions?

1 Which country hosted the first World Cup in 1930 and went on to win the competition?

2 A closely-fought 2-2 draw against which country secured England's place at the 2002 World Cup finals?

3 Which midfielder scored France's third goal in their 3-0 World Cup final win over Brazil in 1998?

4 In which country were the 1982 World Cup finals held?

5 In which year was Gary Lineker the competition's top scorer with six goals?

6 Which England star had a header disallowed in England's second round meeting with old foes Argentina at France '98?

7 How many times have Brazil won the World Cup?

8 Which legendary Italy striker missed the decisive penalty in the 1994 World Cup final shoot-out?

9 Which England striker scored a hat-trick in the final of the 1966 World Cup?

10 Which Turkey star scored the fastest ever World Cup goal after 10.8 seconds in Japan & Korea?

11 And which Toon Army star scored England's first goal at the France '98 finals?

1 POINT PER CORRECT ANSWER

WORDFIT

Fill in the names of these world-class strikers into the grid below so they all connect. France's David Trezeguet starts you off!

TREZEGUET

CRESPO
DEL PIERO
ELBER
FOWLER
HENRY
HESKEY
KLUIVERT
LARSSON
LOPEZ
MORIENTES
OWEN
RAUL
RIVALDO
RONALDINHO
RONALDO
SAVIOLA
SHEVCHENKO
TREZEGUET
TRISTAN
VIERI

1 POINT PER CORRECT ANSWER (MAXIMUM 20)

THE MAGIC NUMBER

Work out the answers to each question and then insert each correct number into the sum to reveal 'The Magic Number'!

$$A \div B + C \times D + E - F = G$$

A. The shirt number worn by Michael Owen for Liverpool.
B. Number of times Arsenal have won the Premiership title.
C. Margin of England's win over Germany in September 2001.
D. Number of goals scored in the 2002 Champions League final.
E. Number of Football League clubs containing the letter X.
F. The age of England skipper David Beckham.

	÷		+		X	

	+		−		=	

5 POINTS FOR CORRECT ANSWER

LEGS ELEVEN

Which top young stars do these chunky pins belong to?

2 POINTS PER CORRECT ANSWER (MAXIMUM FOUR)

GAFFER FORCE

MATCH puts the world's top managers in the spotlight!

Hi, I'm Marcelo Lippi, and I'm the manager of a top European club – but which one?

2 POINTS FOR CORRECT ANSWER

ROBERT PIRES QUIZ

The Arsenal ace was sidelined for a while through injury, but just how much do you know about the French star?

1 Pires joined Arsenal from which club in 2000?

2 And how much did The Gunners have to pay to secure his services?

3 True or false? Pires was a sub in France's Euro 2000 final win against Italy?

4 The midfielder scored a goal of the season contender in the 2-1 win over which Midlands club?

5 Pires injured his knee against which North East club in the FA Cup?

2 POINTS PER CORRECT ANSWER

SPELL CHECK STARS

We put a host of Premiership stars through a computer spell-check – can you suss out who's who from these three chewed-up remains?

1. Eminent Whiskey
2. Domino Matter
3. Maroon Pharoah

2 POINTS PER CORRECT ANSWER

TRANSFER TRACKER

Which Premiership player's career history is this?

1988-1992 Watford

1992-1999 Liverpool

1999-2001 Aston Villa

2001-present West Ham

2 POINTS FOR CORRECT ANSWER

DAVID BECKHAM England

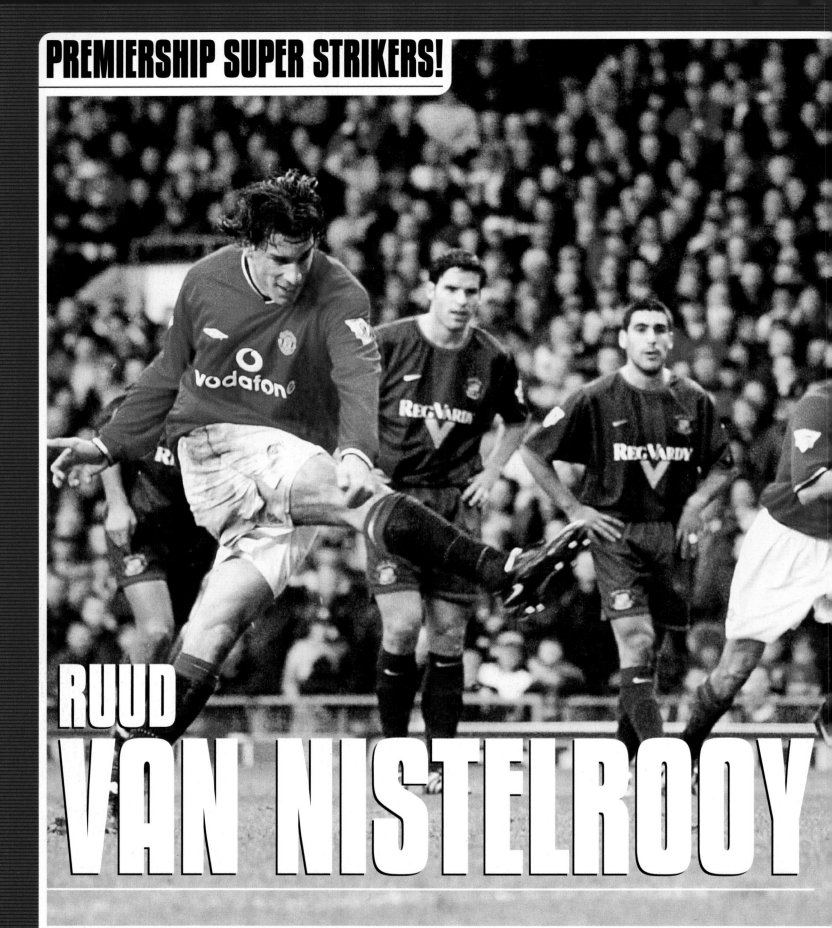

PREMIERSHIP SUPER STRIKERS!

RUUD VAN NISTELROOY

RUUD VAN NISTELROOY TIMELINE...

SEPTEMBER
BOSCH BOY
Wins his first professional contract with Second Division FC Den Bosch.

JANUARY
TOP MAN
Makes the step to the Dutch top flight with SC Heerenveen.

JULY
PSV PAY BIG
Dutch giants PSV Eindhoven pay a Dutch record for the striker.

NOVEMBER
DUTCH DELIGHT
Finally makes his international debut with Holland.

MAY
PLAYER POWER
Voted Dutch Player Of The Year by his fellow professionals.

DECEMBER
TOON TRY
His ex-PSV manager Bobby Robson tries to bring Ruud to Newcastle United.

1993   **1997**   **1998**   **1999**

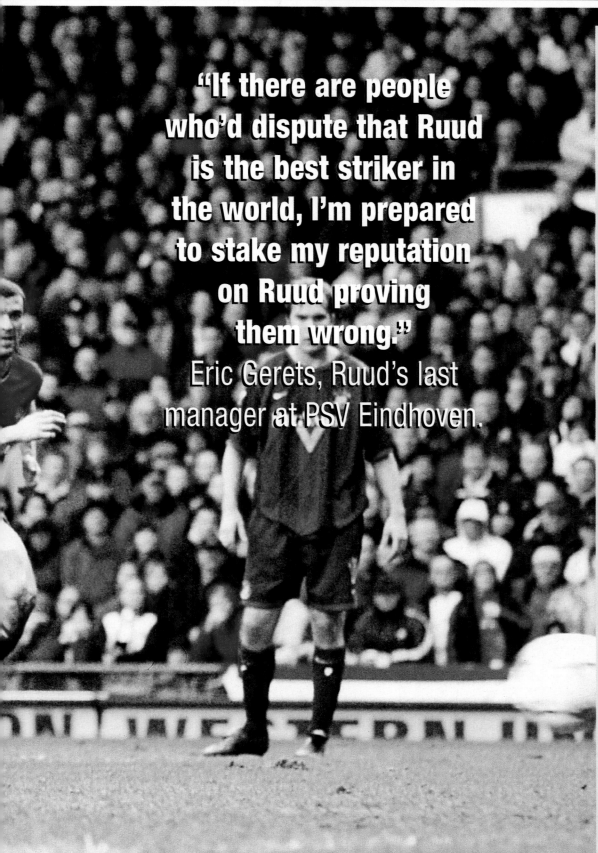

"If there are people who'd dispute that Ruud is the best striker in the world, I'm prepared to stake my reputation on Ruud proving them wrong."
Eric Gerets, Ruud's last manager at PSV Eindhoven.

See how the Ruud boy rose to the top of the pile against all the odds!

Traditionally, all the great Dutch players have come from the north of Holland, where the rich clubs from towns like Amsterdam and Utrecht find and develop young talent. But Ruud van Nistelrooy is definitely not a traditional player. His roots are in the south of the country – where cycling is more popular than footy – and he didn't have the famous youth system at Ajax to help him to greatness. He did it through hard work, and a massive helping of natural striking talent.

He started his career with his village side, but from there his determination to succeed in the game saw him progress step by step to professional football in the Dutch Second Division. Although the world didn't know it at the time, from then on it had a brand new star. In fact, Van Nistelrooy got so far he eventually made it on to the cover of MATCH, but how did the star striker travel from such humble beginnings to the very peak of footballing achievement? Read on, and let us explain…

CAREER FACTFILE

Born: July 1, 1976 in Oss, Holland

Nationality: Dutch

Position: Striker

Height: 6ft 3ins

Weight: 12st 8lbs

Former clubs: FC Den Bosch, SC Heerenveen, PSV Eindhoven

Signed: From PSV Eindhoven for £19 million on April 23, 2001

Man. United debut: v Liverpool on August 12, 2001

Total Man. United games/goals: 49/34 (August 2001 to May 2002)

International caps/goals: Holland 18/8 (November 1998 to July 2002)

APRIL
NO KNEE'D
A freak collision in a friendly against Silkeborg weakens cruciate ligaments.

MANC MISERY
His £19 million move to Manchester United is called off due to his damaged knee.

SNAP SHOT
Collapses in training as his ligaments finally give way.

JUNE
EURO KO!
Watches Euro 2000 from his hospital bed in America.

2000

MAY
UNITED MAN
Manchester United finally sign the striker now he's fit.

AUGUST
FIRST BLOOD
Scores on his debut in the Charity Shield.

FRIENDLY FIRE
Notches against England in a 2-0 friendly win.

2001

JANUARY
GREAT EIGHT
Completes a record eight goals in consecutive Premiership games.

2002

APRIL
PLAYERS' PLAYER
Gets the ultimate stamp of approval when fellow professionals vote him PFA Player Of The Year.

1987

LOCAL TALENT!

Ruud's the son of two footballing parents, so it's no surprise that he started playing young. His first team was his local village outfit Nooit Gedacht (which translates in Dutch as 'Never Thought Of It') and he was a great success there, apart from the fact that he didn't score many goals – because, bizarrely, he was played as a sweeper!

It was at the age of 17 that Ruud got his break into the big time, and the club that gave him his first chance in the pro game was a Dutch Second Division side called FC Den Bosch. Soon, there were rumours going round that the club had their hands on a youngster who could finally match up to the Dutch striking legend Marco Van Basten (left).

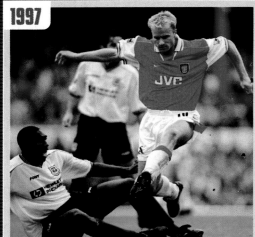

1997

HEERENVEEN HE COMES!

It was January 1997 when SC Heerenveen came in for Ruud. No, they might not be the most glamorous club in Europe, but it got the Ruud boy in the shop window. While he was there, his club told him to watch Dennis Bergkamp play to improve his own game, so Ruud regularly made the long trip to London to study the Dutch master.

It soon started paying off, as he scored an impressive 13 goals in 30 appearances. That prolific rate didn't go un-noticed, and it wasn't long before the next step on the long road to success was complete, because in 1998 PSV Eindhoven signed him. What's more, they paid £4.2 million – a Dutch record at the time – for the up-and-coming striker.

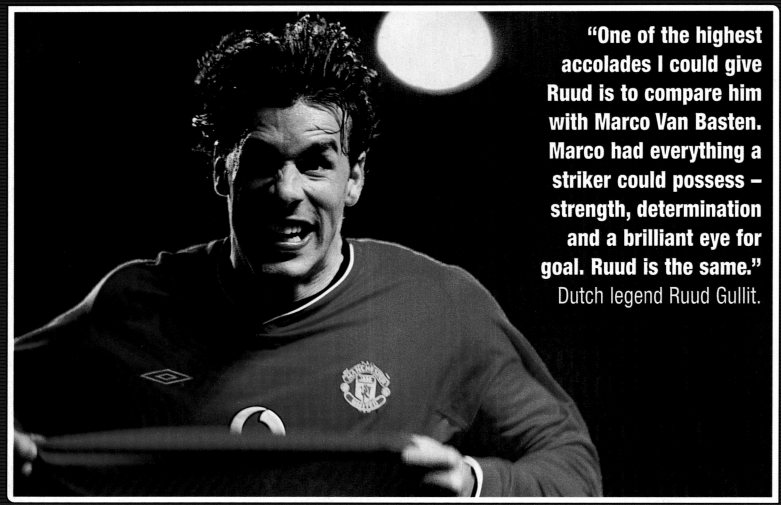

"One of the highest accolades I could give Ruud is to compare him with Marco Van Basten. Marco had everything a striker could possess – strength, determination and a brilliant eye for goal. Ruud is the same."
Dutch legend Ruud Gullit.

1998

INTERNATIONAL DEBUT WITH HOLLAND!

November 18, 1998 was a very special day for young Ruud – it was the day he first pulled on the famous orange shirt of the Holland senior international team. The occasion was a high drama friendly against bitter rivals Germany, and although Ruud didn't score in the game, he certainly made his mark on the match, forcing a fine point-blank save from German 'keeper Oliver Kahn. The Holland team had just unearthed a future international diamond!

1999

TOP OF THE CHARTS!

May 1999 saw the end of Ruud van Nistelrooy's first season at PSV, and guess what? He finished as top scorer! The 31 goals he banged in had finally confirmed him as one of the most prolific marksmen in the whole of Europe, and gave him second place in the European Golden Boot Awards. There was still one question mark over Ruud though – he had finished as the Dutch league's top scorer, but would he be able to prove himself in one of the tougher leagues in Europe? To be a truly great player, Ruud knew he had to make his mark in a league like the Premiership, La Liga or Serie A.

2000

APRIL RUUD DEVIL!

Manchester United manager Alex Ferguson certainly thought the young striker could make it at the very highest level, and in April 2000, the footy world was hit with the sensational news that Ruud was on his way to the Premiership. And the deal came so close to being completed that a Press Conference had even been called – but at the very last moment, it collapsed. Why? The Manchester United medical team had decided that Ruud's knee wasn't strong enough after a clash he'd suffered earlier that month. More bad news followed, as two days later his knee gave way while trying to prove his fitness and he was laid up with cruciate ligament damage.

2000

MAY LIGHTNING STRIKES TWICE

At the end of the 1999-2000 season, Van Nistelrooy had again finished as PSV's top goal-getter. It was a fairly impressive record on its own, but it was even more amazing when you consider the details of it. Firstly, the Ruud boy spent two months of the campaign injured, and so missed out on the chance to score in about ten games. Secondly, he managed to score two superb hat-tricks against Dutch giants Ajax – one in each of the home and away fixtures – so if anyone needed proof that he could score against the best, surely this was it. Look out world!

2000

JUNE EURO HEART-ACHE

Euro 2000 was supposed to be Ruud's first chance to shine at an international tournament, but because of the injury, there was obviously no way he could take part. He didn't actually miss out on winning the tournament – as Holland lost out to Italy on penalties in the semi-final – but the boys in orange could have really done with his services that summer. He did make one appearance which had the nation cheering for him, though. From his hospital in America where he was getting treatment, he waved his crutches to cheer one of Holland's Euro 2000 goals. Top man!

2001

BACK TO BLIGHTY!

Ruud spent the whole of the following year working on his knee. First he went to America to visit the world's best knee surgeons. Next, he slowly went about building up the strength until he could walk on it, and then running until his scoring sharpness had returned at last. Thankfully, he came back the same player he'd been before his injury, and by March he was back scoring goals again for PSV. Before you could say 19 million, the Man. United deal was back on the table. This time it went through, and Ruud fulfilled his childhood dream of playing for the great Manchester United.

2002

JANUARY STRIKE A LIGHT!

Was Alex Ferguson right to shell out £19 million for a striker who might still have been crocked? Well, yes, as it turned out. On January 19, 2002 Van Nistelrooy completed one of the most amazing feats a striker has ever achieved. Not only did he score in eight league games in a row, he actually scored in ten consecutive matches – one of the extra goals was in the Champions League, the other in the FA Cup. On top of that, his Manchester United team won all those games, taking them back to the top of the table. Ruud bagged one hat-trick, two braces and 14 goals in 10 games. Get in!

2002

MAY PERFECT PFA!

Manchester United might not have won any trophies last season, but that wasn't for a lack of effort on Ruud's part. His sensational showing in front of goal made him one of the big stars of the 2001-02 season, and the campaign did finish with one high – Van Nistelrooy was awarded the PFA's Player Of The Year Award. The accolade is one of the most highly regarded in the game, because it's not some random panel of know-it-all footy journalists which decides the winner – it's the players themselves. So don't just take our word for it, listen to what the players have said – Ruud is the best!

"Say hello to Mr Football, Stevie."

Get it down ya, son!

I can see right down your tracky top!

GERRARD'S GOT THE POWER!

Training in the heat is no problem for Stevie G – but it is for Planet Footy!

Before the 2002 World Cup, the one thing on Steven Gerrard's mind was getting fit for South Korea & Japan. Sadly, a groin injury destroyed that dream for the Liverpool midfielder, but just before it happened, MATCH caught up with the star to find out exactly how he was preparing for the heat and humidity.

With temperatures in Asia reaching a scorching 85ºF, with 85 per cent humidity all through June, Gerrard had to make sure he would be hydrated at all times. So with the help of isotonic sports drink Powerade, Stevie was put through his paces in a specially-heated sports hall – working out how much fluid he sweated away and how long he could keep going on the exercise machines!

First up was some light cycling – doing 10km in the heat. **"I'm knackered already!"** he laughed after five seconds, before plugging on with the task! He was sweating all over the place, but still seemed full of energy. Afterwards, Stevie weighed himself to see what the effect was. It turns out that over a 90 minute game, the midfielder loses 2.7 per cent of his body weight – which is 2.2kg!

Gerrard then took a little break, while he did an interview with TV's little presenting princess Lisa Rogers – who had done the same workout in her red tracksuit, with Planet Footy's ace reporter enjoying the sight of her getting all sweaty!

After that, it was back to yet more exercises for Stevie, with Liverpool's demanding coaching staff, and then finally a series of five-a-side games. He was still going strong right to the end though, so the Powerade was obviously working wonders.

But by that point, our reporter had collapsed in the heat, soaking wet in sweat and gasping for air. It was a good job he wasn't called up to the World Cup to replace Stevie G, wasn't it?

The Liverpool coaches tell Stevie to get on his bike!

You couldn't really see down my top, could you?

Gerrard had to wear a bib – in case he dribbled!

MATCH

WORLD SUPERSTARS

RAUL Spain

>FOOTY MAD!<

WE'VE GONE CAPTION CRAZY!
There's always room for a laugh at someone else's expense – as this selection of MATCH pics shows!

Becks is in the spotlight so much, he has to put his shades on!

Book the linesman ref, he's taken a dive!

Who said the only silverware at Man. City was in the canteen?

"Yes! The gaffer's said I can drive the coach home!"

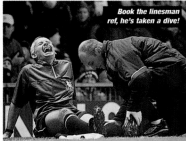

David Platt always did talk a good game.

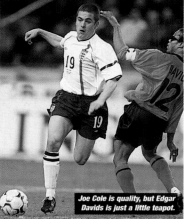

Joe Cole is quality, but Edgar Davids is just a little teapot.

"Okay ball, do as I say and we'll get along just fine."

Liverpool coach Phil Thompson is always sticking his nose in other people's business.

Wee John Collins proves he's still got a spring in his step.

"This is how I scare the birds away in my garden, Deano."

Celtic striker John Hartson celebrates another goal.

Guess who won Southampton's piggyback race this year?

"The toilet's up there, you say? Right, I'll be back in ten lads."

Graham Poll directs the midfield traffic.

"Sorry Steven, what was that? My Scouse is not too good."

"Of course I remember what the First World War was like."

WORLD SUPERSTARS

MATCH

RONALDO Brazil

THE GREATEST TEAM ON EARTH!

Which players would make up the perfect XI? MATCH gets thinking and puts together the best team on the planet!

Imagine the Earth had to play a Galaxy XI for the survival of the human race! Who would you pick? Who'd be your star striker? Who'd have the safest hands in goal? What formation would you go for? They're tough questions which aren't easily answered. For every great player you put in, there are hundreds you're leaving out. How do you choose between Figo, Zidane, Rivaldo, Beckham, Totti, Mendieta, Vieira and Veron, and still get the right balance? Well, MATCH took on the challenge!

First, we chose the formation and picked our dream line-up. We looked at each position in the team and chose the best man for the job. We then worked out our who our dream manager would be, who would be skipper and who'd take all the set-pieces. Nothing has been left down to chance. We've created the ultimate outfit on this planet, ready to kick some intergalactic ass should the day come! Welcome to the Greatest Team On Earth...

THE GREATEST TEAM ON EARTH - THE CONTENDERS!

GOALKEEPERS

Who's the number one No.1? The world's most expensive 'keeper is Italy's Gianluigi Buffon, worth a huge £30 million at the age of 24 and agile, cool and confident. Another youngster with a great future is Iker Casillas of Spain. The 21-year-old has everything you need and, with time, he will surely get to the top – but not yet. At the other end of the age scale there's David Seaman, but the pony-tailed veteran is too old to zimmer-frame his way into our team. Turkey's Rustu Recber is up there, as is Jerzy Dudek of Poland, Shay Given and Fabien Barthez. Sadly, the most impressive 'keeper around is still Germany's Oliver Kahn. His experience, agility, presence and big mouth make him the perfect goalie!

SELECTIONS
- Oliver Kahn

CENTRE-BACKS

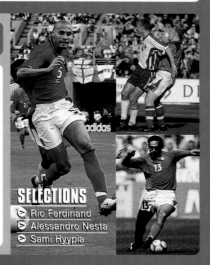

The centre-backs almost pick themselves here! Rio Ferdinand, newly crowned as the world's best central defender, is a dead cert. Alessandro Nesta of Italy is widely regarded as another talented performer – a classy centre-back like Rio who can bring the ball out of defence. Alongside them, you need a hard man. Lilian Thuram hasn't impressed in the past year, Igor Tudor is injury-prone, Marcel Desailly's not always up for it, Jaap Stam's too slow, Sol Campbell too clumsy, Samuel Kuffour not consistent enough, and Kevin Hofland too young. So it's a battle between Walter Samuel of Argentina and Finland's Sami Hyypia. In the end, it has to be Hyypia, as he is just that little bit scarier!

SELECTIONS
- Rio Ferdinand
- Alessandro Nesta
- Sami Hyypia

WING-BACKS

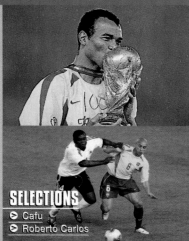

The wing-back positions need two players who are going to get up and down the flanks all day. This is not one of the stronger areas in world footy, with a lack of genuine wide men. Bixente Lizarazu has been up there for years, but time is starting to catch up with him – as it is with Paolo Maldini. Vincent Candela, another Frenchman, Romanian Cosmin Contra and Japan's Shinji Ono have all looked good. You'd be hard-pushed to find a weakness in Javier Zanetti, Argentina's right wing-back, but his place is taken by the irresistible bundle of Brazilian energy, Cafu! To complement him, Roberto Carlos is called up on the left flank, to give energy and attacking flair on both sides of the team!

SELECTIONS
- Cafu
- Roberto Carlos

MIDFIELDERS

How can you squeeze the world's best midfielders into just three? It's not easy. You'll need one defensive midfielder who can break up the attacks, and Roy Keane, Emerson of Brazil, Steven Gerrard, Paul Scholes and Mark Van Bommel of Holland fit the bill. However, the undisputed champ here is Patrick Vieira. For the two creative midfielders, Figo and Zidane are kings, but to keep a balance, you'd only take one. It has to be Zidane. The third midfielder needs to have attacking flair, a good engine and a willingness to track back. Pavel Nedved, Luis Enrique and Michael Ballack are all contenders, but David Beckham just pips Nedved and United team-mate Ryan Giggs.

SELECTIONS
- Patrick Vieira
- Zinedine Zidane
- David Beckham

STRIKERS

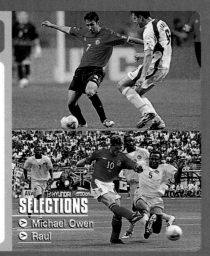

A good strike partnership is as much down to getting the right combination as having the best players, and that means an out and out striker and another who'll drop off. For the deeper striker, Francesco Totti and Alex Del Piero spring to mind, as do Argentina's Javier Saviola, Ronaldinho, Alvaro Recoba of Uruguay and Patrick Kluivert. Eventually, it's between Raul and Rivaldo, and Raul takes it – just! As for the predator, it's hard to find a player with everything. Andrij Shevchenko almost has it, and Ronaldo looks like he's back, but there are question marks over both. Ruud van Nistelrooy's close, as are Thierry Henry and Christian Vieri. But, for sheer pace and instinct, Michael Owen takes it!

SELECTIONS
- Michael Owen
- Raul

MANAGER

The world's greatest bosses tend to be in club management, with the likes of Sir Alex Ferguson, Arsene Wenger and Sir Bobby Robson outstanding in England. In Italy, Hector Cuper, Marcelo Lippi and Fabio Capello have fine reputations. In Germany, Ottmar Hitzfeld has enjoyed much success with Bayern Munich, and who can forget Klaus Toppmoller at Bayer Leverkusen? On the international front, no coach stands head and shoulders apart, except for our choice of manager – Sven Goran Eriksson. Sven's enjoyed success throughout his managerial career, winning the title in Portugal, Sweden and Italy, but his job of transforming England is his outstanding achievement. Sven's boss!

GAFFER
- Sven Goran Eriksson

TACTICS

With an abundance of attacking talent, it's vital the defence is solid, and the Brazilian duo of Roberto Carlos and Cafu offer the perfect balance between defence and attack. To cover their runs, you need three centre-backs with a tough-tackling midfielder in front. This frees the attacking quartet to get forward, though they need to drop back and help out if needed! If the team was chasing a goal, Rivaldo would replace Hyypia and play in left midfield in a 4-4-2 formation.

ROLES

For the fantastic job he does for England, David Beckham is the perfect captain of the World XI. He leads by example, and with such an array of talent in the side, you need a big personality with drive when the going gets tough. As well as taking the armband, Becks will also be responsible for taking corners and will share free-kicks with Zidane and Roberto Carlos. And with Raul named as the side's penalty taker, you'd better hope you don't concede any spot-kicks!

OLIVER KAHN

> Goalkeeper
> Germany

The 33-year-old, hilariously nicknamed 'The White Gorilla' by German fans, built up such a reputation that England's fantastic 5-1 victory in Munich was as much a shock because he conceded five goals as it was the actual result. Big, commanding, agile and full of self-confidence, Kahn is from the same school as Peter Schmeichel. His reputation is still such that in every one-on-one, his aura makes him seem to grow in size. At the peak of his powers and with many years left, defenders must love him as the last man.

ON THE SUBS BENCH...

> Gianluigi Buffon

The world's most expensive 'keeper and a huge presence between the sticks.

RIO FERDINAND

> Central Defender
> England

Rio was always going to be a star, ever since he appeared as a youngster for West Ham way back in 1995. Since then, a British record £18 million move to Leeds and the chance to play in the Champions League really gave him the confidence to make the step up to a world-class performer. Tall, elegant and quick but with an imposing physique, Rio took the 2002 World Cup by storm and hasn't looked back. He's been compared to the late Bobby Moore and if he fulfils that promise, there's no limits to what he can do!

ON THE SUBS BENCH...

> Lilian Thuram

His reputation took a knock at the World Cup but Thuram is still a star performer.

SAMI HYYPIA

> Central Defender
> Finland

Sami Hyypia is like a 20-foot statue carved out of granite – except he's a lot more mobile. When the Finnish international came to Liverpool, few people knew much about him. But strikers soon found out who he was, when he shut them out for match after match. With his dominating style, Hyypia has become the rock on which Gerard Houllier's Liverpool side have built their success. If Hyypia played for one of the big football nations, he'd be a massive star – and any team in the world would want him.

ON THE SUBS BENCH...

> Walter Samuel

Unlucky to miss out, as he is a quick, powerful and determined competitor.

ALESSANDRO NESTA

> Central Defender
> Italy

Everything about Nesta is slick – his defending, his passing, his hair... Nesta is an idol in Italy, as he's everything they admire – a stylish defender in the mould of all the great Italian centre-backs. Like Rio Ferdinand, he's always dominant in the air, strong in the tackle, quick over ground, and more than comfortable when bringing the ball out of defence. His injury problems were probably the main reason for Italy's early elimination from the 2002 World Cup, but when Nesta's fully fit, he's as good as it gets!

ON THE SUBS BENCH...

> Fabio Cannavaro

Nesta's defensive partner for Italy and a competitive and classy act to boot.

CAFU

> Right wing-back
> Brazil

The Roma fans call him 'Pedolino' after the Italian express trains, because of his speedy overlapping runs going forwards! It's a good nickname, but it doesn't do Cafu justice – coz if the opposition spring an attack after one of his surging runs, the player you'll see breaking up the attack at the other end will be Cafu again. He might not be the best defender in the world, but his play going forward and energy make up for it. The Brazil skipper has over 100 caps and would have got into any Brazil team ever!

ON THE SUBS BENCH...

> Javier Zanetti

The Argentinian pushes Cafu close, for his forward runs and strong defending.

ROBERTO CARLOS

> Left wing-back
> Brazil

Carlos is a little thunderball full of energy and power. His runs from left-back have made him the most feared attacking defender in the world today, and his shooting is legendary. He got his enormous thighs from working on the farm pulling ploughs through dry ground in Brazil. As a result, Carlos can run 100 metres in 10.2 seconds and hit the ball harder than anyone else going! He may not always hit the target with his barnstorming free-kicks, but he has the skills and tricks to make him a lethal attacking option!

ON THE SUBS BENCH...

> Vincent Candela

The flamboyant Frenchman is equally comfortable in going forward or defending.

PATRICK VIEIRA

> Midfield
> France

Vieira is perhaps the most coveted player in world football right now – and during the 2001-02 season at Arsenal, you could see why. But why would Real Madrid want the France star for £40 million? Well, perhaps it's his ability to totally dominate a game from the start, protecting the back four and starting up attacks. Perhaps it's his ability to come out of any tackle, whether 50-50 or 1-99 against him, with the ball at his feet. Whatever the reason is – as David Ginola once smarmed, 'ee eez worth eet!

ON THE SUBS BENCH...

> Roy Keane

The original Terminator and probably the most determined player in world football.

ZINEDINE ZIDANE

> Midfield
> France

Zidane lives on a different planet to us mortals. The Real Madrid star has been elevated to a distinguished group of football legends, including Michel Platini, Diego Maradona, Pele, Johan Cruyff, Bobby Moore, Eusebio, Ferenc Puskas, George Best and Garrincha. Everything Zidane does is brilliant – his shooting, his passing, his dribbling – even his heading. But most of all, it's his first touch. Zidane caresses the ball like no other player in the world can, or ever has. Enjoy him while he's still playing!

ON THE SUBS BENCH...

> Luis Figo

Out of form for a while, but when he's hot, he can destroy any team around.

DAVID BECKHAM

- > Midfield
- > England

International superstar David Beckham could be straight out of a Hollywood blockbuster – every stage of his life seems to be a fairytale! On the pitch, he's put his ability to good use, becoming Man. United's main man and England's inspirational captain. He sometimes doesn't boss games like he could, but he makes up for that with his shooting. Beckham's got control of his temper, and turned his right foot into a magic wand. With all that, and his will to win, you've got a player who can achieve anything.

ON THE SUBS BENCH...

> Pavel Nedved

The Czech star, like Beckham, makes the most of his ability and gives 110 per cent.

RAUL

- > Striker
- > Spain

The Prince of football has achieved almost everything there is to achieve in club football three times over! At first glance, Raul isn't exceptional. He's not quick, he's not overly strong, he isn't tall – but he's a player without peers. His eye for goal is awesome, he makes countless goals for others, and his reading of the game is exceptional. For Madrid, it's said that if he wanted to, he could easily get the club president or manager removed. Raul's a leading light for Spain and closing in on their record goals tally. And he's only 25…

ON THE SUBS BENCH...

> Rivaldo

Perhaps the world's most gifted player, Rivaldo can win a game at the drop of a hat.

MICHAEL OWEN

- > Striker
- > England

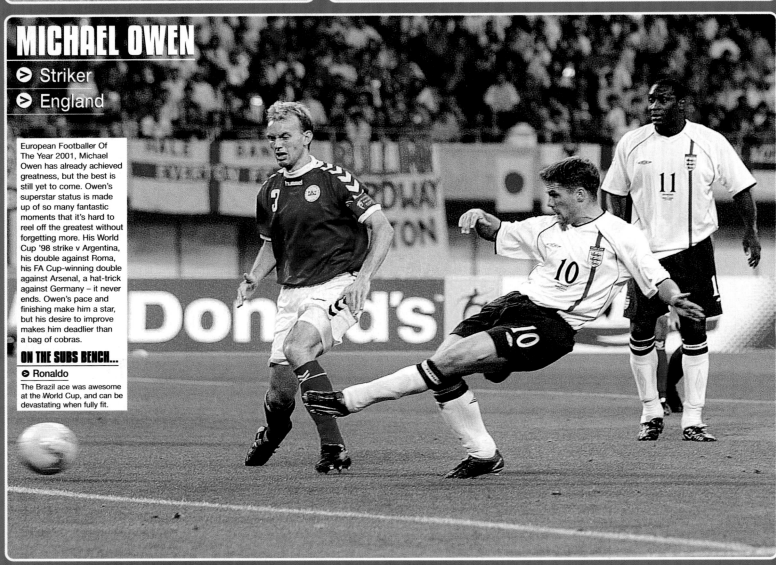

European Footballer Of The Year 2001, Michael Owen has already achieved greatness, but the best is still yet to come. Owen's superstar status is made up of so many fantastic moments that it's hard to reel off the greatest without forgetting more. His World Cup '98 strike v Argentina, his double against Roma, his FA Cup-winning double against Arsenal, a hat-trick against Germany – it never ends. Owen's pace and finishing make him a star, but his desire to improve makes him deadlier than a bag of cobras.

ON THE SUBS BENCH...

> Ronaldo

The Brazil ace was awesome at the World Cup, and can be devastating when fully fit.

KAHN

HYYPIA

NESTA

CAFU

FERDINAND

CARLOS

BECKHAM

VIEIRA

ZIDANE

RAUL

OWEN

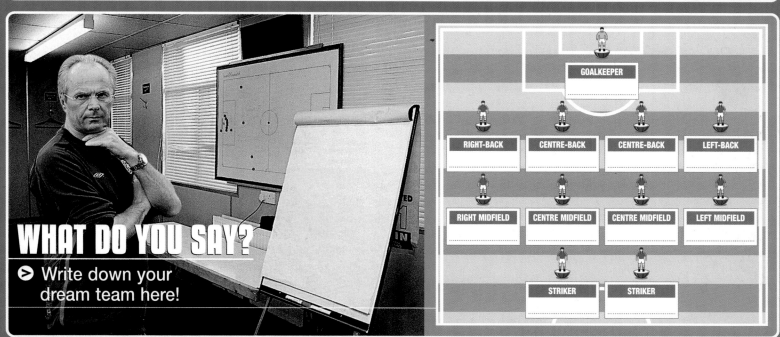

WHAT DO YOU SAY?

➤ Write down your dream team here!

GOALKEEPER

RIGHT-BACK

CENTRE-BACK

CENTRE-BACK

LEFT-BACK

RIGHT MIDFIELD

CENTRE MIDFIELD

CENTRE MIDFIELD

LEFT MIDFIELD

STRIKER

STRIKER

Sir Bobby Robson – who did he sign for Barcelona?

Second XI

They're the ones you see ranting on the touchline, but just how much do you know about managers?

1 While manager at Barcelona, which Brazilian striker did Bobby Robson sign from PSV Eindhoven?

2 Liverpool's Gerard Houllier originally joined the club as joint manager. Who did he work alongside?

3 Which manager led Birmingham City out of Division One and into the Premiership for the first time?

4 Who was in charge of Derby on the day they got relegated from the Premiership last season?

5 Name the coach in charge of the Italian national team at the 2002 World Cup.

6 Which club did David Moyes leave to join Everton near the end of last season?

7 Who was manager of Man. United before Alex Ferguson arrived from Aberdeen?

8 Which Turkish club did Blackburn boss Graeme Souness manage earlier on in his career?

9 Who replaced Ruud Gullit as Chelsea boss when he was sacked in 1998?

10 Who was the Fulham boss between Kevin Keegan and Jean Tigana?

11 How many full-time managers did the England team have during the 1990s?

1 POINT PER CORRECT ANSWER

FREAK
OR
UNIQUE!

True or false?
Man. United's Fabien Barthez performs this shorts-ripping ritual before every match.

2 POINTS FOR CORRECT ANSWER

KIT KINGS

Which poor team had to turn out to play in this pile of old cow pat?

2 POINTS FOR CORRECT ANSWER

BALL GAMES

Starting at No.1, fill in the answers (the last letter of each answer is the first letter of the next), complete the circle and re-arrange the yellow letters to reveal a legendary Brazil striker.

1. Colombian who starred for Aston Villa in 2001-2002.
2. Italian winners of the European Cup Winners' Cup in 1999.
3. Southampton striker who was snapped up from Blackpool.
4. Danny, the West Brom striker previously at Sunderland.
5. Nigeria's skilful midfielder, Jay-Jay, now at Bolton.
6. Sulky French striker who signed for Man. City in May 2002.

10 POINTS FOR CORRECT ANSWER

anegrams

Rearrange the letters to find five top Arsenal stars!

1. VA MAN IS DEAD
2. AVIS TORN WILDLY
3. AIR PICKIER VAT
4. ALB COP SMELL
5. ACHE SOLELY

2 POINTS PER CORRECT ANSWER

Those Were The Days

Chelsea celebrate winning the Cup Winners' Cup in 1998, but who scored the only goal of the game?

3 POINTS FOR CORRECT ANSWER

SPELL CHECK STARS

We put a host of stars through a computer spell-check and came up with these remains – but who are they?

1. Nicholas Ankle
2. Jonny Inmate
3. Mark Fallback
4. Delia Adobe
5. El Hag Roof

2 POINTS PER CORRECT ANSWER

SAY WHAT?

Just who is television pundit Gary Lineker talking about here?

He could eat an apple through a tennis racket!

2 POINTS FOR CORRECT ANSWER

EYE EYE!

Can you identify these five top Premiership stars just by gazing into their eyes?

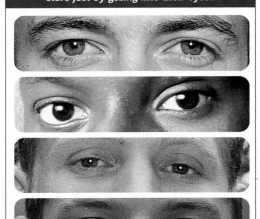

2 POINTS PER CORRECT ANSWER

MATCH

DAMIEN DUFF Republic Of Ireland

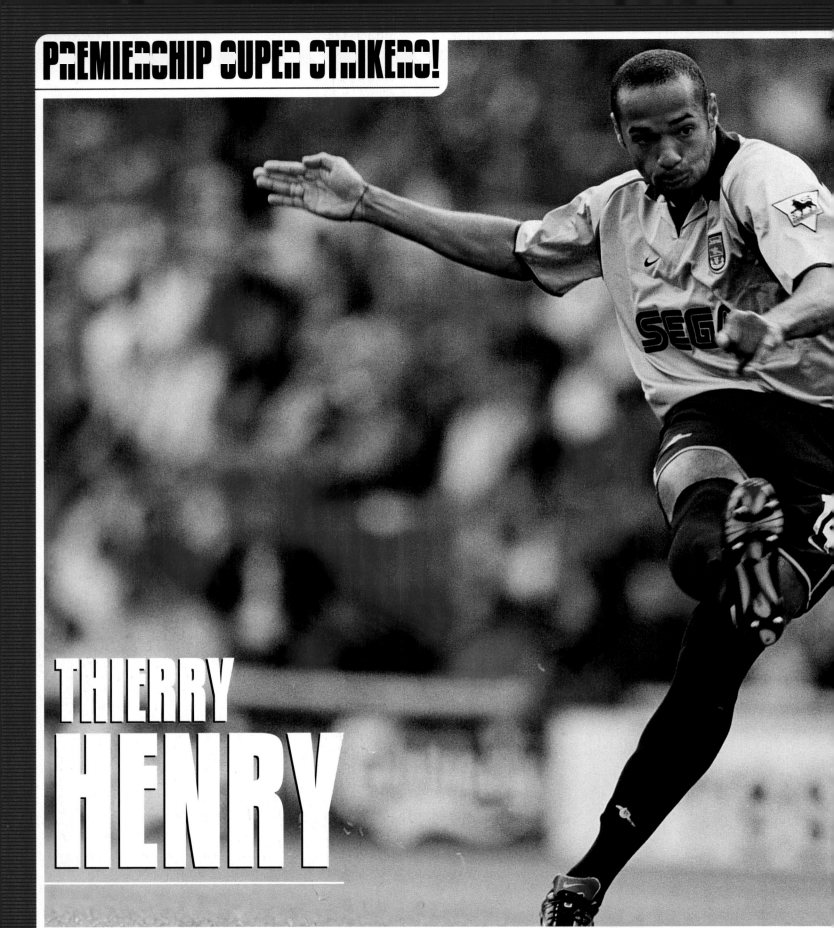

PREMIERSHIP SUPER STRIKERS!

THIERRY HENRY

THIERRY HENRY TIMELINE...

SEPTEMBER
HERE WE GO!
Launches career with the Monaco youth set-up at the age of 13.

1990

JULY
STAR STOCK
Already a rising star, Henry's made captain of the France Under-18 team.

1994

AUGUST
NICE DEBUT SON!
On August 31 1994, at 17 years old, Wenger gives Titi his chance in the Monaco team with a league game against Nice.

1995

JUNE
CHAMPIN' AT THE BIT!
Wins the European Under-19 Championships in France, for France!

1996

OCTOBER
FRENCH FANCY
Wins his first cap for France on October 11 against South Africa.

1997

NOVEMBER
EURO WARNING
Scores two goals on his Champions League debut against Sporting Lisbon.

> **"I was watching a youth game – a Paris derby between Ulis and Palaiseau. One player scored five goals and stood out by a mile. His name was Thierry Henry."**
> Thierry's first ever coach, Jean Marie Panza.

MATCH reveals how Thierry rose from Paris back streets to fame!

Unless you've been hiding in a dark cave for the last three years or so, the name Thierry Henry will instantly conjure up images of skill, flair, style, and above all, goals! Yup, since Arsene Wenger bought the promising winger from Juventus, Thierry's gone from strength to strength, and he's now sitting pretty as one of the most dangerous strikers in Europe. And rightly so, too!

You see, Wenger saw something in the young Frenchman that his other coaches hadn't noticed. Instead of playing in his usual position on the wing, he saw that Henry should be an out-and-out centre-forward, because while he was effective out wide, it wasn't his best position. Titi, as Henry's mates call him, has never looked back, but how did he become one of Europe's hottest properties?

MATCH looks back at an ultra-successful career that has taken Thierry Henry from the back streets of Paris to the pinnacle of world football with Arsenal and France.

CAREER FACTFILE

Born: August 17, 1977 in Paris
Nationality: French
Position: Striker
Height: 6ft 2ins
Weight: 13st 1lb
Former clubs: Monaco, Juventus
Signed: From Juventus for £10 million on August 6, 1999
Arsenal debut: v Leicester City, August 7, 1999
Total Arsenal games/goals: 149/80 (August 1999 to May 2002)
Trophies won at Arsenal: FA Barclaycard Premiership 2002, FA Cup 2002
International caps/goals: France 38/12 (October 1997 to September 2002)

1998

APRIL
JUVE YOUTH
Scores for Monaco against his future club Juventus in the European Cup.

JULY
WORLD WONDER
Wins the World Cup with France at the age of just 21.

1999

JANUARY
TURIN' AROUND
Makes a big-time move to Italian Serie A giants Juventus.

AUGUST
HIGHBURY HIGH
Arsene Wenger is reunited with the striker as Thierry moves to Arsenal.

2000

MARCH
LEFT FOR RED
UEFA Cup disaster for Henry as he's red-carded against Werder Bremen.

DECEMBER
HAT-TRICK HAPPY
Scores his first hat-trick in England against Leicester City in the Premiership.

2001

MAY
FA CUP UPSET
Plays in his first FA Cup final – against Liverpool – but loses 2-1.

JULY
ASIA ACE
Wins the Confederation Cup – a warm-up event for the World Cup – with France.

2002

DECEMBER
HIGH TOON
Henry blows his top against Newcastle and has to be escorted off.

MAY
TROPHY TIME
24 league goals and a fine FA Cup display help win the Double with Arsenal.

JUNE
FRANCE FLOP
A bad miss and a red card are all Henry gets out of the World Cup.

1987

THE FIRST STEP

Thierry set off on his football career by signing schoolboy forms with local club Versailles. He grew up in a pretty rough Paris suburb where there was only one way to keep out of trouble – and that was to play for the local club. Titi got in with a side called Les Ulis – and that's where his football education really started – but Versailles was his first real break.

Of course it was hardly Paris St Germain, but Thierry knew that getting attached to any of the organised clubs out there would help him achieve his one wish – to be one of the world's biggest footy stars. And how right he was, because by the age of 13 he was snapped up by French giants Monaco!

1994

EUROSTAR!

Thierry didn't have to wait long before a debut at his new club! On August 31, 1994, at the age of just 17, he was drafted into the first team by coach Arsene Wenger, and while his mentor was soon to move to Japanese side Grampus Eight, Henry still managed to play eight games in the first team that season.

That got his profile right up in France, and before long he'd become a member of France's youth teams. Under the guidance of Gerard Houllier (left), France went on to win the under-19 European Crown two years later, giving Thierry his first taste of complete and utter European domination.

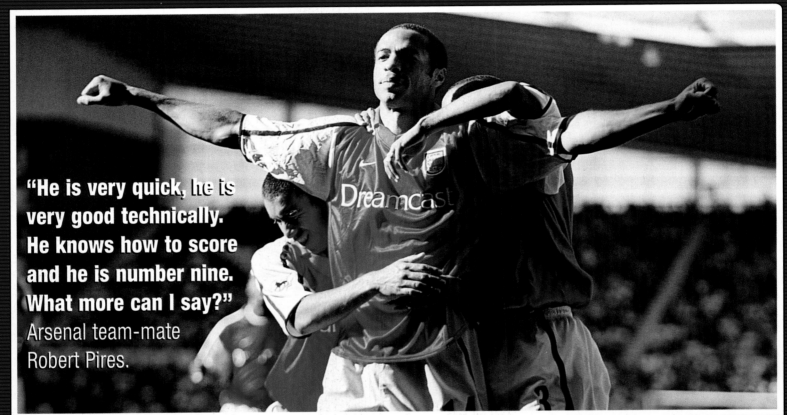

"He is very quick, he is very good technically. He knows how to score and he is number nine. What more can I say?"
Arsenal team-mate Robert Pires.

1997

MARCH HENRY'S UEFA CUP BOW!

Thierry was soon back to playing football on the European stage, as the Monaco team he was playing for charged their way through to the semi-finals of the UEFA Cup. Henry's blistering pace down the wings was soon causing even the very best European defences trouble, and it was at the quarter-final stage when Thierry really made his first mark on English fans.

Monaco were drawn against Newcastle United, and an Henry-inspired performance ended in a 3-0 win which, considering they'd already won the first leg 1-0 away, was some victory. Everyone who saw those games knew they'd seen the future of European football on show – a lightning quick lad called Thierry Henry.

1997

MAY TITLE NO.1!

Monaco were finally knocked out of the UEFA Cup by Inter Milan, but Henry's influence on the team did lead to silverware that season. As one of the hottest young talents in French footy, the flying Thierry helped propel Monaco to the French league championship under the guidance of yet another future Premiership manager, Jean Tigana.

It was an achievement that wasn't lost on Europe's biggest clubs, and even the most optimistic Monaco fan knew they wouldn't be able to hold on to their young superstar forever. Rumours were starting to spring up all over the place about where Thierry was going to go next, but he was determined to be loyal to the club that'd given him his big chance for as long as possible.

1998

WORLD WINNER!

Ask any player what the pinnacle of their career would be and they would all give you the same answer – and that's to win the World Cup. So just imagine how proud Thierry Henry would have been to represent his country at the 1998 tournament, on home soil, at the age of just 21. Then try to imagine how you'd feel if you went on to win the trophy at such a young age!

Well, for Henry it was more than dreams, because in the summer of 1998 that's exactly what happened. He didn't play in every game, but he still managed to score two goals as yet again he was up to every challenge that was put before him. He even netted in the penalty shoot-out as Italy were dumped out!

1999

JANUARY JUVE BOUND!

After proving to the world that he could cut it on the biggest stage of them all, Henry became top of every European side's wish list, and it was certain he would go to one of the biggest clubs. In 1999, a dream bid came in from Italian giants Juventus, and there was no way that club or player could say no. Marcello Lippi, then Juve manager, made no secret of his desire to have Henry's pace down the wing, and that's where he played him. But it wasn't the most productive spell of Thierry Henry's career, and although he managed to score three goals in 16 games, he wasn't at his best.

The move wasn't everything he had expected it to be, and with all the pressure the Italian supporters and media piled on, he was soon looking for a way out. Was he thinking about events in England, where Arsene Wenger had won a Premiership and FA Cup double with Arsenal? He could have been, you know...

1999

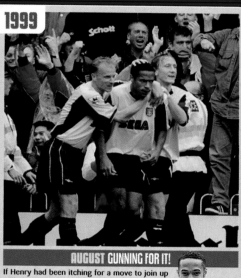

AUGUST GUNNING FOR IT!

If Henry had been itching for a move to join up with ex-Monaco coach Wenger, his dream came true on August 1, 1999 when he officially became a Gunner. The north London club had just won the double thanks to the goals of Nicolas Anelka, but Thierry's compatriot had just left the club so the responsibility on the new boy's shoulders was huge.

It didn't start as well as he would have hoped, as Henry went his first eight games without a goal. Wenger stuck with him as a striker though, and after the first goal went in against Southampton, they kept on coming.

2000

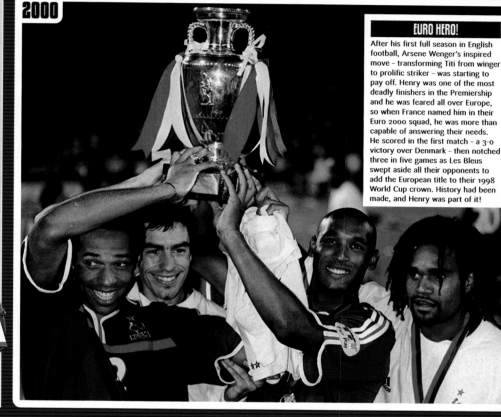

EURO HERO!

After his first full season in English football, Arsene Wenger's inspired move – transforming Titi from winger to prolific striker – was starting to pay off. Henry was one of the most deadly finishers in the Premiership and he was feared all over Europe, so when France named him in their Euro 2000 squad, he was more than capable of answering their needs. He scored in the first match – a 3-0 victory over Denmark – then notched three in five games as Les Bleus swept aside all their opponents to add the European title to their 1998 World Cup crown. History had been made, and Henry was part of it!

2002

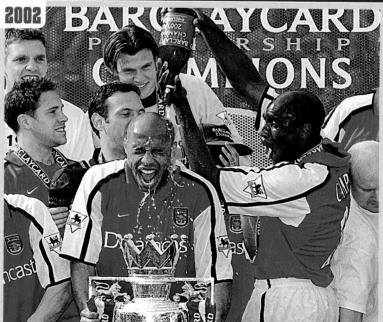

MAY DOUBLE TROUBLE!

Considering Thierry joined The Gunners in 1999, it's amazing to think he didn't win anything with them until the 2001-02 season. But when the trophies started coming, they came with one hell of a bang. Not only did Arsenal win the league by seven points from Liverpool, and a full ten points from Man. United, they also beat Chelsea 2-0 in the FA Cup final. Thierry's name will go down in Highbury history as the striker who won the Premiership Golden Boot with 24 goals to clinch an historic third league and cup double!

2002

JUNE WORLD CUP WOE!

All the talk before the 2002 World Cup in South Korea & Japan was of France being the red-hot favourites to win the trophy for the second time in a row. Surely all they had to do was turn up, strut their stuff, and it was theirs for the taking. Not so.

Their first game was against the unfancied Africans of Senegal, but they lost 1-0, and Thierry missed a sitter in the second half. Worse was to come though, as in the second game – a vital game against Uruguay – a lunatic lunge earned Thierry a red card and a suspension for the next game, which turned out to be France's last. Henry would soon be back though – did you ever doubt it?

DID YOU KNOW?

Michael Owen's favourite subject at school was geography - well, the Liverpool striker definitely knows where the goal is, doesn't he?

THE KNOWLEDGE

BRAZILIAN FOOTBALLERS' NICKNAMES...

1 The habit of calling players by their nicknames is as Brazilian as samba! They do this to avoid putting something like Edson Arantes do Nascimento on the back of shirts, which was Pele's real name!

2 Dunga, captain of the 1994 World Cup-winning team, was so-called because school pals said he looked like one of the dwarves from 'Snow White'. In Brazil, Dunga means 'Dopey'!

3 Juninho turned into Juninho Paulista when he returned to Brazil from Middlesbrough, because there was another Juninho at his new club Vasco da Gama. Paulista means he's from Brazilian city São Paulo. He was alright though, as the other Juninho became Juninho Pernambucano!

4 You wouldn't be happy if you were nicknamed 'Beleza' in Brazil. It means 'good looking', but they use it for ugly players! Ugly and rubbish players are nicknamed 'Cara de Jegue', meaning 'donkey face'!

5 Former Brazil striker Müller was so-called because he reminded everyone of great German striker and all-time record World Cup goalscorer Gerd Müller! Not a bad compliment!

6 Many Brazil players are given nicknames that reflect what they look like. Tostao, a little player from the 1970 World Cup, was named after a small Brazilian coin. Garrincha, a World Cup winner in 1958 and 1962, was called 'little bird'.

7 Roberto Carlos is named after a singer! His mum was a big fan of Roberto Carlos – the Brazilian Robbie Williams!

8 When Ronaldo burst on to the Brazil scene, there was an older player with the same name. So they called the buck-toothed star Ronaldinho – meaning 'Little Ronaldo'!

9 When the new, David Seaman-lobbing Ronaldo arrived, they had a problem, so the older Ronaldo became Ronaldão – or 'Big Ronaldo' – buck-toothed Ronaldinho became Ronaldo, and the new guy became Ronaldinho! Complicated, eh?

10 Pele doesn't even mean anything! the name was given to him at school, but at home he was nicknamed Dinho. And at his first club, he was nicknamed Gasolina. Weirdo!

THE Numbers GAME
SPOTLIGHT ON: REAL MADRID

3
The number of British coaches Real Madrid have had. First up was Arthur Johnson (1910-20), then it was Michael Keeping (1948-52) and John Toshack (1989-91 & one more season in 1998).

9
Real's record number of European Cup wins. They were champions in 1956 and won it for the next four years on the trot! After two wins in the 1960s, they also won in 1998, 2000 & 2002.

10
There were ten goals scored in 1960 when Real beat Eintracht Frankfurt 7-3! The game sealed their fifth European Cup win in a row, with Puskas scoring four and Di Stefano notching three.

45
The number of minutes that the 1998 Champions League semi-final between Real and Borussia Dortmund was held up – after some loony fans pulled down one of the goals at The Bernabeu!

80
28 league titles, 17 Spanish Cups, nine Euro Cups, two UEFA Cups, one League Cup, six Spanish Super Cups, two Inter-continental Cups, one Copa Latina, two Little Cups and 12 regional titles. Phew!

105,000
The capacity of the Santiago Bernabeu. It's named after a lawyer, who'd been a Real player, manager and president, as well as being part of the Real side that dominated Europe in the 1950s!

-£120,000,000
Real's bank balance in pounds at the start of 2000-01. The debt nearly wiped out the club, but fans said they would boycott Madrid banks if the money lenders demanded their dosh back!

£175,000,000
The amount Real sold their training ground for in 2001, wiping off all their debts and paying for the purchase of Zinedine Zidane! The local council, run by Real Madrid fans, bought the site!

MICHAEL OWEN'S WIND-UP OF THE WEEK!

Oi lads, you know about Stevie G?

Eh?

He's so thick, right...

Shut up Michael.

...that he has a ruler by his bed to see how long he sleeps!

Nah I don't!

You're so easy to wind up!

Git.

RIO FERDINAND England

"I'VE HAD AN AB

Ever missed a sitter and wished the ground would swallow you up? Don't

ASHLEY COLE *ARSENAL*

"My most embarrassing moment was when I got hit by something from the crowd during the Albania game. I went down like I'd been shot! It turned out to be a lipstick case, and I got a lot of grief for that! I didn't know what it was as I didn't see it afterwards. I thought it was a bottle and it cut my forehead, nose and lips – it wasn't just lipstick on my face! – and it did hurt. It was my debut and I don't think about it much, but it was pretty embarrassing."

ADE AKINBIYI *CRYSTAL PALACE*

"I think I must have been quite lucky, because there's not anything that really sticks out. The only time I've done anything really stupid was when I made my debut for Norwich. I went to warm up but went running the wrong way! Instead of running out where the referee is, because that's where you're supposed to go, I went running off the other way. Suddenly all the crowd and the boys were laughing at me, so that was really embarrassing."

DARREN HUCKERBY *MAN. CITY*

"It was when I was first starting out at Lincoln and I was sub for a first-team game. I was only about 18 and I got booked without even getting on the pitch. I had a fight with Terry Hurlock, the big fella who used to play for Millwall! I had a bit of a tussle with him. It was late on in the game, I was warming up and he wanted me to pass the ball back to him quick but I just left it, so we had a bit of a fracas. He was a big lad, so I was away sharpish after the game!"

MAGNUS HEDMAN *COVENTRY CITY*

"Mine was when I was playing for AIK Solna away to Sparta Prague. It had been 0-0 at home and there were ten minutes left in the game. I came out to punch the ball, but hit it straight into the back of their striker. The striker had turned away, and when he felt the ball hit him, he turned back and put the ball into the empty net. But two minutes after I made one of the best saves of my career, so it was quite a strange match for me all in all."

JASON DODD *SOUTHAMPTON*

"I'm lucky in that I've not had too many, but in one of my first games for The Saints I was meant to put Deep Heat on my legs to warm them up, but I put the wrong stuff on. It was Algipan, which absolutely killed, and my legs were bright red! Algipan's just like Deep Heat but a lot hotter. It's meant to help your muscles but I didn't realise it was so strong. That was one of my worst moments – when I went out on the pitch with bright red, burning legs!"

SETH JOHNSON *LEEDS UNITED*

"There's already been too many! I missed a sitter on Sky against Southampton when I was at Derby. It was a header from about a yard out and I managed to put it 16 yards wide! Then there was the time when I took a corner for Crewe and knocked it straight into touch along the floor. I didn't even get it off the ground, it just went straight out along the floor! We were 3-0 down at home at the time so that didn't go down too well with the lads."

MATT HOLLAND *IPSWICH TOWN*

"I remember my shorts ripped on my debut for Bournemouth against Huddersfield. It was only about two minutes after the kick-off and they got completely ripped in a tackle and were flapping all over the place! The bench called me over and I had to take them off right in front of the crowd. I was only 20 and got loads of wolf whistles! Fortunately, I had some decent underwear on and wasn't wearing a thong or anything – that would have been a nightmare!"

STEVE WATSON *EVERTON*

"Own goals are always embarrassing if you're unfortunate enough to score them. Luckily I haven't scored many in my time, but one was at Old Trafford a couple of seasons ago which has to be the worst place of all to get one. The worst thing was, it was a very important game for them. After that, I got loads of Manchester Manchester United fans coming up to thank me while I was walking round the village I live in near to Birmingham, and I really hated that!"

RICHARD SHAW *COVENTRY CITY*

"I've been pretty lucky in that I've not had too many embarrassing moments in my career, but there's one incident that does stick in my mind. I was a young lad playing for Crystal Palace against Chelsea down at Stamford Bridge, and I somehow managed to score an own goal at The Shed End about two minutes into the game. If that wasn't bad enough, they started singing my name after that for the entire game, so that was very embarrassing for me!"

CHRISTIAN DAILLY *WEST HAM*

"I was a 17-year-old playing for Dundee United. I was sitting on the bench when the manager told me I was going on. I got warmed up and I was about to take my warm-up top off when I realised I didn't have a strip on! I just sprinted down the tunnel to get one. I didn't say a word to anyone and I don't think they knew what I was doing. They were saying, 'Where have you been?' I said, 'I just had to nip inside', but the worst thing was, I never got on."

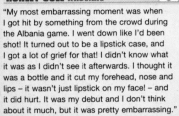

SOLUTE 'MARE!"

worry, some of the top stars' most embarrasing moments are far worse!

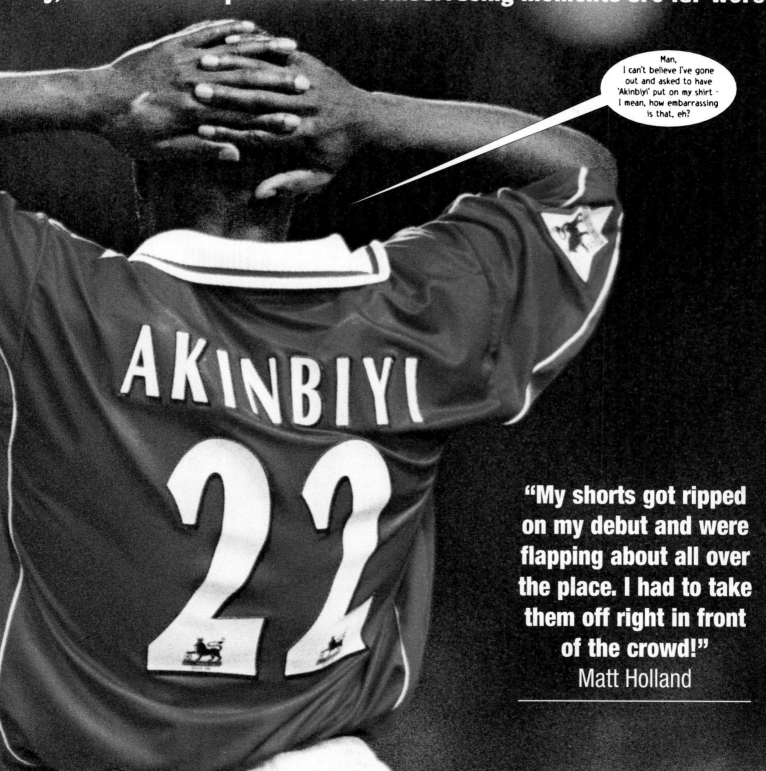

Man, I can't believe I've gone out and asked to have 'Akinbiyi' put on my shirt – I mean, how embarrassing is that, eh?

"My shorts got ripped on my debut and were flapping about all over the place. I had to take them off right in front of the crowd!"
Matt Holland

Stevie Mac – a European Cup winner with Real.

third XI

The European Cup is the greatest club competition around, but how much do you really know about it?

1 Which Spanish giants won the first ever European Cup way back in 1956?

2 True or false? Liverpool have won the European Cup a total of five times.

3 Which was the last Italian club to win the trophy in 1996 – Juventus or Bologna?

4 Valencia finished runners-up in consecutive years recently, but which years were they?

5 How many winners medals does Steve McManaman have with Real Madrid – is it a) 2, b) 5 or c) 6?

6 Do FA Cup winners go into the UEFA or European Cup draw?

7 True or false? Nottingham Forest have won the trophy twice in their history.

8 Champions League games are shown on which television station - ITV or BBC2?

9 How many points do you get for a win in the group stages of the competition - is it a) 2, b) 3 or c) 4?

10 In which year did Sir Alex Ferguson help guide Manchester United to the European Cup?

11 Young England midfielder Owen Hargreaves has already won the European Cup playing for which top European side?

1 POINT PER CORRECT ANSWER

CAP IN HAND

He was a living legend of a striker for many of years with Liverpool and Wales, but how many international caps did Ian Rush win during his brilliant career?

a) 53

b) 63

c) 73

3 POINTS FOR CORRECT ANSWER

ALPHABET QUIZ

The answers to all of these questions begin with the letter 'H'.

1. Ruud van Nistelrooy plays for this international side.
2. The first name of this Real Madrid star is Ivan, but what's his surname?
3. Glasgow Stadium where Scotland play their international home games.
4. The player who moved from Leicester to Liverpool for £11 million in 2000.
5. This young England midfielder plays his club football with Bayern Munich.

2 POINTS PER CORRECT ANSWER

WHO AM I?

Which young Everton star is being congratulated here after scoring?

2 POINTS FOR CORRECT ANSWER

GOALMOUTH SCRAMBLE

See how many words you can make, of three or more letters, from the surname of Spurs defender Dean Richards.

D S R I R C A H

1 POINT PER CORRECT ANSWER (MAXIMUM 15)

STEVEN GERRARD QUIZ

He's the Liverpool and England ace who's one of the top midfielders in the world, but how much do you know about Steven Gerrard?

1 The tough-tackling star has been around for a few years now, but just how old is Stevie Gerrard?

2 True or false? Injury ruled the young midfield dynamo out of England's 2002 World Cup squad.

3 In which year did Steven make his Premiership debut for Liverpool – was it a) 1998, b) 1999 or c) 2000?

4 Gerrard made his England debut in 2000 against which country?

5 And how many times did Stevie G play for the England Under-21s?

2 POINTS PER CORRECT ANSWER

TRANSFER TRACKER

Which Premiership player's career history is this?

1986-1992 Nantes

1992-1994 Marseille

1994-1998 AC Milan

1998-present Chelsea

3 POINTS FOR CORRECT ANSWER

SPELL CHECK STARS

We put these international stars through a computer spell check and got these chewed up remains. Can you suss out who they are?

1. Henna Crisps
2. Rivalled
3. Fillip Incise

2 POINTS PER CORRECT ANSWER

WORLD SUPERSTARS

ALESSANDRO DEL PIERO Italy

50

TOP PREMIERSHIP PLAYERS OF 2001-02!

Presenting the top 50 players of last season, as exclusively rated by MATCHfacts!

The Premiership's been the most exciting league in the world for years now, but last season gave us more thrills than ever! Man. United were expected to walk it, especially after signing Juan Sebastian Veron and Ruud van Nistelrooy. But Arsenal had other ideas, with Robert Pires named the Football Writers' Player Of The Year as The Gunners marched to their first title since 1998. Liverpool gave them a run for their money though, while Newcastle surprised everyone by finishing fourth.

But which player topped our MATCHfacts ratings? Who performed week in, week out for their club? These are the most accurate ratings you'll ever find, because we watch every game of the season and we don't rate players by reputation – they have to earn their mark out of ten every week. Now you can find out who's won our prestigious MATCHMAN Of The Season award, as we count down the 50 best players of last season…

PREVIOUS MATCHMEN OF THE YEAR!

1997-1998	1998-1999	1999-2000	2000-2001
Dennis BERGKAMP *Arsenal*	**Tony ADAMS** *Arsenal*	**Paolo DI CANIO** *West Ham*	**Ryan GIGGS** *Man. United*

In MATCHfacts, everyone who plays more than 15 minutes in a game is awarded a rating out of ten and the best player from each side is given a star rating. Players must have played at least 15 games in the 2001-02 season to be in the running for the MATCHMAN Of The Season award – the ultimate reward for excellence in every game!

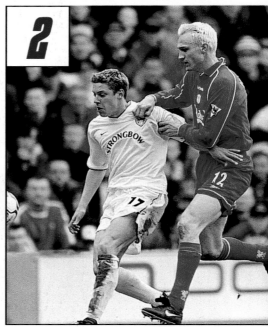

ROY KEANE
Manchester United

Age: 31 ★ **Position:** Midfielder

Lowdown: Whatever you think about Roy Keane, you can't deny his importance to Man. United. The Red Devils are a great team, but they always look better with their skipper in the side. New boy Ruud van Nistelrooy might have won the PFA Player Of The Year award in his first season, but Keano was the driving force behind the side. An outstanding total of ten MATCHfacts star ratings in 28 games says everything about his contribution – and an awesome average of 7.57 blew the opposition away to lift the 2001-02 MATCHMAN Of The Season award.

MATCHFACTS RATINGS		
PLAYED	STARS	AVERAGE
28	10	7.57

> Why did he have such a good season, then?
On a personal level, Roy Keane had a fantastic season. The image of his goal in the Champions League semi-final second leg against Leverkusen will stick long in the fans' memory, as the captain tried to take United through to the final almost single-handedly. But, despite his own impressive form, the midfielder will tell you last season was a disaster, because United didn't win anything.

> So how come they didn't manage to pick up a trophy?
There's only so much one man can do, and unfortunately for Keano and Man. United he was let down too often by his team-mates. Man for man, United should have walked to their eighth Premiership title in ten years, but other high-profile stars didn't pull their weight. Don't believe us? Just look at the stats – from United's star-studded team, only four of them made our top 50 list, and only Keano was in the top ten.

> What about Keano's famous temper, though?
Surprisingly, the United hard man only picked up four yellow cards and one red in 28 Premiership games for The Red Devils. Having said that, the red card was for trying to floor Alan Shearer with a fantastic-looking right hook in the 4-3 defeat at Newcastle.

> So what can we expect from Keano in the future?
Roy Keane will demand improvement from his team-mates, but he'll want to maintain the stunning consistency he achieved last season. After being sent home from Ireland's World Cup camp he's had to ignore the critics, get his head down and concentrate on what he does best. Keano signed a new deal last season which should keep him at Old Trafford until 2005. There has been talk of ending his career with an emotional move to Celtic, but Keane was suspended for United's Champions League triumph in 1999 and you get the feeling he's still got some unfinished business.

SAMI HYYPIA
Liverpool

Age: 29 ★ **Position:** Defender

Lowdown: In turning Liverpool into Premiership title contenders again, Sami Hyypia has been one of the club's most inspirational buys. The Big Finn only missed one game last season, and he picked up seven star ratings in keeping The Reds solid at the back. He was named captain after Jamie Redknapp's departure to Spurs – reflecting his growing influence on the team – and there was no more consistent defender in the Premiership. Considering his power in the air, he'll want to improve his tally of three goals from last season, but he'll be pleased with only three bookings from 37 games, which meant he never missed a game through suspension. Finishing as runner-up to Roy Keane in our MATCHMAN Of The Season award is also a big improvement on last year's sixth-place finish.

MATCHFACTS RATINGS		
PLAYED	STARS	AVERAGE
37	7	7.29

3

ROBERT PIRES
Arsenal

Age: 28 ★ **Position:** Midfielder

Lowdown: What a season the Arsenal star had. Before March he couldn't put a foot wrong, with regular stunning strikes and defence-splitting passes. Bobi quickly became arguably the best player in a mightily talented team, and he was winning praise from the football world – until disaster struck. On March 23, the left-winger lined up for an FA Cup Sixth Round replay against Newcastle at Highbury. After a routine challenge from Nikos Dabizas, the Frenchman fell to the ground with screams of agony. No-one would have wished his cruciate knee ligament injury on him, and after a truly brilliant season, the player who was looking forward to setting the World Cup alight faced a long, long road to recovery.

MATCHFACTS RATINGS		
PLAYED	STARS	AVERAGE
28	5	7.22

4

RIO FERDINAND
Leeds United

Age: 24 ★ **Position:** Defender

Lowdown: Has any player in the Premiership improved as much as Rio in the last 18 months? Probably not. After moving to Leeds, the former West Ham man fulfilled his potential to become the perfect defender. He's even more comfortable on the ball now, he can pass or bring the ball out of defence like a midfielder, and is rarely beaten in one-on-ones. In moving from 29th place last year to fourth, Ferdinand has also cemented himself as England's first-choice centre-back and was the star of The Three Lions' World Cup campaign. Niggling injuries kept him out of seven Premiership games last season, but on the field, the Leeds captain went 31 games without getting booked.

MATCHFACTS RATINGS		
PLAYED	STARS	AVERAGE
31	7	7.16

5

STEED MALBRANQUE
Fulham

Age: 22 ★ **Position:** Midfielder

Lowdown: When the £5 million Belgian-born French midfielder arrived at Craven Cottage last summer from Lyon, most Fulham supporters hadn't heard of him. But Malbranque soon caught the eye with his craft and guile, not only feeding strikers Louis Saha and Steve Marlet, but scoring eight goals from 37 Premiership games himself.

MATCHFACTS RATINGS		
PLAYED	STARS	AVERAGE
37	10	7.13

6

JOE COLE
West Ham United

Age: 21 ★ **Position:** Midfielder

Lowdown: Joe Cole just gets better every season, and for the second year running he's made the top ten of our list. Under Glenn Roeder, he finally got the central midfield responsibility he craved – and his skill demanded. He didn't score in 30 league games, but Joe's creating more chances for his team-mates and the goals will definitely come.

MATCHFACTS RATINGS		
PLAYED	STARS	AVERAGE
30	8	7.13

7

DAMIEN DUFF
Blackburn Rovers

Age: 23 ★ **Position:** Midfielder

Lowdown: The skilful winger was Blackburn's star last season as they climbed away from the relegation zone towards mid-table. The Republic Of Ireland man was a bag of tricks on the left, bamboozling defenders and scoring some vital goals. After ten star ratings and a fantastic World Cup, he was regularly linked with a big-money move.

MATCHFACTS RATINGS		
PLAYED	STARS	AVERAGE
32	10	7.12

8

KIERON DYER
Newcastle United

Age: 23 ★ **Position:** Midfielder

Lowdown: He may have only played 18 games for the Toon last season, and critics could point out that he only scored two goals, but when Kieron Dyer took the field for Bobby Robson's team he was worth two extra players. As usual, Dyer's blend of pace, skill and endless energy got the better of nearly everyone he played. And get this: of the 18 games he played last season, Newcastle lost only two – that's a sensational record. It underlines just how important Dyer is to The Magpies, and it makes you wonder just what he could have done for them if he'd been fit for the whole season.

MATCHFACTS RATINGS		
PLAYED	STARS	AVERAGE
18	4	7.11

9

GARETH SOUTHGATE
Middlesbrough

Age: 32 ★ **Position:** Defender

Lowdown: Clearly unhappy at Aston Villa at the end of the 2000-01 season, Southgate moved to Middlesbrough and began to enjoy his football again. Gaz got a whopping 12 star ratings – more than anyone else in our top 50 – and became an instant Riverside hero. He missed just one game for Boro, and was never yellow-carded.

MATCHFACTS RATINGS		
PLAYED	STARS	AVERAGE
37	12	7.10

10

THIERRY HENRY
Arsenal

Age: 25 ★ **Position:** Striker

Lowdown: Another of Arsenal's French Foreign Legion, Henry was almost an ever-present last season and blimey, did he make his presence felt. His 24 goals were enough to see him finish with the Premiership's Golden Boot, and whether it was tap-ins or 25-yard screamers, Titi's talent was up to the task. Henry doesn't earn his place just from his goals though – his tireless running and willingness to get back and win the ball mean he's an asset in more ways than one. With his pace and energy, he just seemed to be everywhere all the time last season - a real gem!

MATCHFACTS RATINGS		
PLAYED	STARS	AVERAGE
33	4	7.06

11

RUUD VAN NISTELROOY
Manchester United

Age: 23 ★ **Position:** Striker

Lowdown: After completing his injury-threatened £17.5 million transfer to Man. United, Dutch ace Ruud van Nistelrooy set the Premiership on fire last season. An impressive total of 23 goals earned him the PFA Player Of The Year award, and the only surprise was that – despite his awesome firepower – United ended the season trophy-less.

MATCHFACTS RATINGS		
PLAYED	STARS	AVERAGE
32	3	7.06

12

STEPHANE HENCHOZ
Liverpool

Age: 27 ★ **Position:** Defender

Lowdown: Commonly known as the 'other half' of Liverpool's rock solid centre-back pairing, Stephane Henchoz was one of the main reasons why The Reds only conceded 30 goals last season. The Swiss defender just refuses to let strikers past, and he's still the most under-rated player in the team - except in Gerard Houllier's eyes.

MATCHFACTS RATINGS		
PLAYED	STARS	AVERAGE
37	4	7.05

13

BRAD FRIEDEL
Blackburn Rovers

Age: 31 ★ **Position:** Goalkeeper

Lowdown: Blackburn signed Brad Friedel from Liverpool on a free transfer in November 2000 – and what a bargain he's proved to be. The experienced USA stopper missed just two league games during the season as he chalked up an average of 7.05 to become our highest-ranking 'keeper. He also helped Rovers to win the League Cup.

MATCHFACTS RATINGS		
PLAYED	STARS	AVERAGE
36	7	7.05

14

GUDNI BERGSSON
Bolton Wanderers

Age: 37 ★ **Position:** Defender

Lowdown: Sam Allardyce was delighted that his defensive rock decided against retiring, as the veteran's steady influence and leadership from the back were key factors in securing Bolton's top-flight status. Bergsson may have collected four 'official' star ratings, but the Iceland man was one of the top performers in every league game last season.

MATCHFACTS RATINGS		
PLAYED	**STARS**	**AVERAGE**
30	4	7.03

15

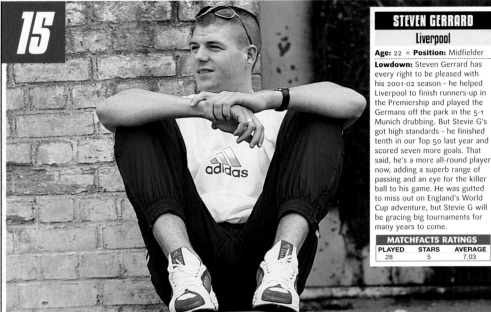

STEVEN GERRARD
Liverpool

Age: 22 ★ **Position:** Midfielder

Lowdown: Steven Gerrard has every right to be pleased with his 2001-02 season - he helped Liverpool to finish runners-up in the Premiership and played the Germans off the park in the 5-1 Munich drubbing. But Stevie G's got high standards - he finished tenth in our Top 50 last year and scored seven more goals. That said, he's a more all-round player now, adding a superb range of passing and an eye for the killer ball to his game. He was gutted to miss out on England's World Cup adventure, but Stevie G will be gracing big tournaments for many years to come.

MATCHFACTS RATINGS		
PLAYED	**STARS**	**AVERAGE**
28	5	7.03

16

PAOLO DI CANIO
West Ham United

Age: 34 ★ **Position:** Striker

Lowdown: Paolo's on-off move to Manchester United may have unsettled him, but the Italian proved his professionalism by continuing to do the business for The Hammers, scoring nine Premiership goals and providing countless assists. Unpredictable and temperamental he may be, but at Upton Park, they just can't get enough of him.

MATCHFACTS RATINGS		
PLAYED	**STARS**	**AVERAGE**
26	6	7.03

17

DEAN KIELY
Charlton Athletic

Age: 31 ★ **Position:** Goalkeeper

Lowdown: 2001-02 was another consistent campaign for Kiely. He played in every league game, picked up six star ratings, and only 'keepers Brad Friedel and Jerzy Dudek are ranked higher in our top 50. Charlton let in fewer goals than West Ham last season, who finished in seventh place, and much of the credit for that has to go to Kiely.

MATCHFACTS RATINGS		
PLAYED	**STARS**	**AVERAGE**
38	6	7.02

18

PATRICK VIEIRA
Arsenal

Age: 26 ★ **Position:** Midfielder

Lowdown: As usual, Vieira was Arsenal's most important player last season. He ran the midfield with his world-class tackling and passing, and his consistent displays were a major factor in The Gunners winning the title - no wonder Real Madrid tried to sign him! He got 11 bookings, and a red card against Leicester, but loyal fans will forgive him!

MATCHFACTS RATINGS		
PLAYED	**STARS**	**AVERAGE**
36	4	7.02

19

JERZY DUDEK
Liverpool

Age: 29 ★ **Position:** Goalkeeper

Lowdown: Looking back, it's no wonder that Arsenal tried to sign Jerzy Dudek as back-up to David Seaman last season. But Arsene Wenger failed to agree a deal for the Polish goalkeeper and bought Richard Wright from Ipswich instead. Dudek was an instant success at Anfield, replacing the below-par Sander Westerveld, and his commanding presence in goal was crucial to Liverpool's mean defensive record.

MATCHFACTS RATINGS		
PLAYED	**STARS**	**AVERAGE**
35	4	7.02

20

STEVE FINNAN
Fulham

Age: 26 ★ **Position:** Defender

Lowdown: There are plenty of exciting players at Fulham, but few of them are more valuable than defender Steve Finnan, who has become one of the best right-backs in the business. He played in every Premiership game last term, was voted into the PFA Team Of The Season, and represented the Republic Of Ireland at the World Cup.

MATCHFACTS RATINGS		
PLAYED	**STARS**	**AVERAGE**
38	2	7.00

21

DEAN RICHARDS
Tottenham Hotspur

Age: 28 ★ **Position:** Defender

Lowdown: Eyebrows were raised when Spurs shelled out £8 million to end the chase for Dean Richards, who played four games for Southampton before scoring on his Tottenham debut in the memorable 5-3 defeat to Man. United. He soon became a key figure – strong, technically sound and unlucky not to get a chance with England.

MATCHFACTS RATINGS		
PLAYED	STARS	AVERAGE
28	5	7.00

22

RAY PARLOUR
Arsenal

Age: 29 ★ **Position:** Midfielder

Lowdown: You may not think of Ray Parlour as one of Arsenal's big stars from last season, but you can't deny the contribution he made in their double-winning success. He didn't score in the Premiership, which doesn't look good, but Parlour brings other things to the Arsenal team – like penetrating runs from midfield and 100 per cent commitment. And Gunners fans will remember his brilliant goal in the FA Cup final for many years to come.

MATCHFACTS RATINGS		
PLAYED	STARS	AVERAGE
27	4	7.00

23

CRAIG BELLAMY
Newcastle United

Age: 23 ★ **Position:** Striker

Lowdown: Many critics were surprised when Bobby Robson bought Bellamy from Coventry last summer. But the lightning-fast striker delivered, and before his injury in February, he was regularly earning impressive MATCHfacts ratings. Newcastle suffered when he didn't play, and with his pace, eye for goal and partnership with Alan Shearer, it's not hard to see why!

MATCHFACTS RATINGS		
PLAYED	STARS	AVERAGE
27	3	7.00

24

MART POOM
Derby County

Age: 30 ★ **Position:** Goalkeeper

Lowdown: The Estonian stopper has been one of Derby's leading players since he arrived at Pride Park in March 1997. Poom shone in 15 league games last season, but was sorely missed through injury. If he'd been available on a more regular basis, Derby may not have lost their Premiership status. Regularly linked with moves to bigger clubs.

MATCHFACTS RATINGS		
PLAYED	STARS	AVERAGE
15	3	7.00

25

EDWIN VAN DER SAR
Fulham

Age: 31 ★ **Position:** Goalkeeper

Lowdown: Fulham's £5 million capture of Edwin van der Sar from Italian giants Juventus was mightily impressive and showed the Londoners meant business. He grabbed the first-team jersey from Northern Ireland's Maik Taylor and missed just one game as Fulham secured top-flight football for another season, keeping 14 clean sheets in total.

MATCHFACTS RATINGS		
PLAYED	STARS	AVERAGE
37	2	6.97

26

SOL CAMPBELL
Arsenal

Age: 28 ★ **Position:** Defender

Lowdown: It was the shock of the century when big Sol made the switch from Tottenham to Arsenal before the start of last season, but as soon as business got underway, he was his usual dependable self. Even when he was faced with some idiotic abuse from supposed Spurs supporters, Campbell proved to be a model professional.

MATCHFACTS RATINGS		
PLAYED	STARS	AVERAGE
31	1	6.96

27

FREDDIE LJUNGBERG
Arsenal

Age: 25 ★ **Position:** Midfielder

Lowdown: Fabulous Freddie was a revelation last season for The Gunners. His stats were amazing – he bagged 12 goals in 25 games from midfield! As it came to the all-important run-in – when the team could have lost its nerve – it was Ljungberg's inspirational form that saw Arsenal to the title with goals against Ipswich, West Ham and Bolton, plus the FA Cup Final winner for good measure!

MATCHFACTS RATINGS		
PLAYED	STARS	AVERAGE
25	1	6.95

28

SHAY GIVEN
Newcastle United

Age: 26 ★ **Position:** Goalkeeper

Lowdown: At the start of last season, Steve Harper and Shay Given were neck and neck for the No.1 shirt at Newcastle, but by the end Given was virtually the first name on the team sheet. Crucial saves at crucial times, including a stunning stop against local rivals Sunderland, made him a real match-winner. Just look at his seven star ratings!

MATCHFACTS RATINGS		
PLAYED	STARS	AVERAGE
38	7	6.94

29

PAUL SCHOLES
Manchester United

Age: 27 ★ **Position:** Midfielder

Lowdown: Man. United's ginger ninja enjoyed another effective season at Old Trafford, even if it did end without a trophy. The England star's late runs into the penalty area from deep, and his confidence to test the 'keeper from distance, saw him score eight goals from midfield and cement his reputation as one of the Premiership's top stars.

MATCHFACTS RATINGS		
PLAYED	STARS	AVERAGE
35	4	6.94

30

JUSSI JAASKELAINEN
Bolton Wanderers

Age: 27 ★ **Position:** Goalkeeper

Lowdown: Regular visitors to the Reebok Stadium will already know why Jussi comfortably made our top 50. He missed just two Premiership games – through suspension – and his imposing frame and agility helped secure The Trotters vital points. Some criticise the way he races off his line, but links with a big-money move prove he's rated highly.

MATCHFACTS RATINGS		
PLAYED	STARS	AVERAGE
34	2	6.94

31

NWANKWO KANU
Arsenal

Age: 26 ★ **Position:** Striker

Lowdown: Arsenal needed all their squad to contribute when it mattered last season - and Kanu did just that. He may not have shown the jaw-dropping skill we've become accustomed to, and he probably didn't start as often as he'd like, but his ability to turn a game with one moment of skill remained a vital weapon in Arsenal's armoury.

MATCHFACTS RATINGS		
PLAYED	STARS	AVERAGE
23	1	6.94

32

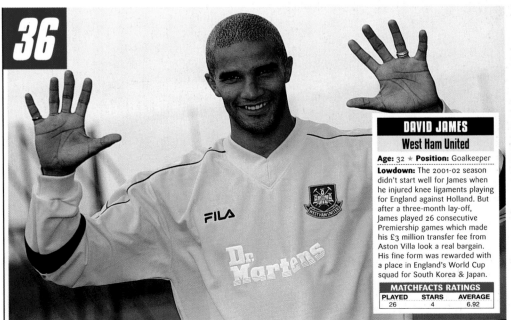

MUZZY IZZET
Leicester City

Age: 27 ★ **Position:** Midfielder

Lowdown: Despite being on the club's transfer list for most of last season, Izzet showed his commitment to Leicester City's cause by turning in top-quality performances week in, week out. Consistently The Foxes' best player, he earned seven star ratings and his top form alerted a host of clubs eager to bring him back to the Premiership.

MATCHFACTS RATINGS		
PLAYED	STARS	AVERAGE
31	7	6.93

33

UGO EHIOGU
Middlesbrough

Age: 29 ★ **Position:** Defender

Lowdown: Dominant in the air and solid as a rock in the tackle, the only negatives of Ehiogu's season were red cards against Arsenal and West Ham. But his form for Boro got him back into the England set-up, and Ugo's central defensive partnership with Gareth Southgate was one of the most impressive in the Premiership last season.

MATCHFACTS RATINGS		
PLAYED	STARS	AVERAGE
29	5	6.93

34

GARY SPEED
Newcastle United

Age: 33 ★ **Position:** Midfielder

Lowdown: A key man in The Magpies' run to the Champions League. Sometimes unnoticed but always influential, Speed's commitment and energy made him a firm fans' favourite. A top performer with four star ratings!

MATCHFACTS RATINGS		
PLAYED	STARS	AVERAGE
29	4	6.93

35

STEVE LOMAS
West Ham United

Age: 30 ★ **Position:** Midfielder

Lowdown: Plagued by a broken toe, but still managed to score four goals after returning to the side early in 2002. Glenn Roeder will have been impressed by his captain's form, which helped West Ham finish seventh.

MATCHFACTS RATINGS		
PLAYED	STARS	AVERAGE
15	3	6.93

36

DAVID JAMES
West Ham United

Age: 32 ★ **Position:** Goalkeeper

Lowdown: The 2001-02 season didn't start well for James when he injured knee ligaments playing for England against Holland. But after a three-month lay-off, James played 26 consecutive Premiership games which made his £3 million transfer fee from Aston Villa look a real bargain. His fine form was rewarded with a place in England's World Cup squad for South Korea & Japan.

MATCHFACTS RATINGS		
PLAYED	STARS	AVERAGE
26	4	6.92

37

CHRIS RIGGOTT
Derby County

Age: 22 ★ **Position:** Defender

Lowdown: One of few Derby players to emerge from the disastrous 2001-02 season with credit. The young centre-back maintained his high standards despite a difficult season in which The Rams were relegated. A tall, ball-playing defender with a bright future ahead of him, Riggott was County's star man nine times from 37 games.

MATCHFACTS RATINGS		
PLAYED	STARS	AVERAGE
37	9	6.89

38

DENNIS BERGKAMP
Arsenal

Age: 33 ★ **Position:** Striker

Lowdown: From almost being a forgotten man during Arsenal's 2000-01 campaign, Bergkamp was back with a bang for The Gunners as they stormed to the Double last season. Some outstanding displays, including seven star ratings, were capped by some truly spectacular goals, none more so than the FA Cup wonder strike against Newcastle.

MATCHFACTS RATINGS		
PLAYED	STARS	AVERAGE
33	7	6.89

39

CARLO CUDICINI
Chelsea

Age: 29 ★ **Position:** Goalkeeper

Lowdown: Despite some fierce competition for the No.1 jersey, the big Italian stopper made it his own. Cudicini came into the side last October, and apart from another four-week absence he was never out of the team again last season. An acrobatic shot stopper, Carlo also saved three penalties - against Ipswich, Sunderland and Liverpool.

MATCHFACTS RATINGS		
PLAYED	STARS	AVERAGE
28	5	6.88

40

BENITO CARBONE
Middlesbrough

Age: 31 ★ **Position:** Striker

Lowdown: Carbone started the season on loan at Derby from Bradford. He played 13 games and scored just one goal there, before moving to Middlesbrough on loan and notching once in 12 games. His creative spark set up countless goals, and Derby's loss was Boro's gain as Beni helped steer Steve McClaren's side well clear of relegation.

MATCHFACTS RATINGS		
PLAYED	STARS	AVERAGE
25	5	6.88

41

TUGAY
Blackburn Rovers

Age: 32 ★ **Position:** Midfielder

Lowdown: The £1.3 million Turk flourished at Rovers, where his cultured passing and long-range shooting thrilled fans. He played in 33 games and formed a good trio with David Dunn and Garry Flitcroft, hitting three goals.

MATCHFACTS RATINGS		
PLAYED	STARS	AVERAGE
33	3	6.87

43

SCOTT PARKER
Charlton Athletic

Age: 21 ★ **Position:** Midfielder

Lowdown: Parker was an ever-present for The Addicks, earning an impressive seven star ratings. Possessing skill and strength, he picked up nine yellow cards and one red, but was still Charlton's top outfield player last season.

MATCHFACTS RATINGS		
PLAYED	STARS	AVERAGE
38	7	6.86

42

RYAN GIGGS
Manchester United

Age: 28 ★ **Position:** Midfielder

Lowdown: Last year's No.1 rated player might have slipped down the pecking order, but it was still another impressive season from the Welsh wonder. Giggs bagged seven goals - a good return from his position out on the left wing - and provided excellent service for the likes of Van Nistelrooy and Ole Gunnar Solskjaer.

MATCHFACTS RATINGS		
PLAYED	STARS	AVERAGE
25	3	6.87

44

JOHN ARNE RIISE
Liverpool

Age: 22 ★ **Position:** Defender

Lowdown: What a spectacular season for the Norwegian who signed for £4.6 million from Monaco last summer. Able to switch from defence to midfield with ease, flame-haired Riise played in all 38 league games for Liverpool and scored seven goals – making him the club's third highest scorer behind Michael Owen and Emile Heskey.

MATCHFACTS RATINGS		
PLAYED	STARS	AVERAGE
38	3	6.86

45

MICHAEL CARRICK
West Ham United

Age: 21 ★ **Position:** Midfielder

Lowdown: West Ham needed a big season from this young midfielder after Frank Lampard's big-money move to Chelsea, and he didn't disappoint the Upton Park faithful. Following his full England debut in May 2000, Carrick continued to impress with his precise passing and tireless work in the middle of the park. A star in the making.

MATCHFACTS RATINGS		
PLAYED	STARS	AVERAGE
30	1	6.86

46

MARTIN KEOWN
Arsenal

Age: 36 ★ **Position:** Defender

Lowdown: The rock-solid and dependable Arsenal man more than proved his worth again last season. Injury kept him out for a fair chunk of the campaign, but the centre-back was a tower of strength at the back for the Double winners. His average MATCHfacts rating of 6.86 from 22 games shows he's still got what it takes, even at 36.

MATCHFACTS RATINGS		
PLAYED	STARS	AVERAGE
22	2	6.86

47

CRAIG SHORT
Blackburn Rovers

Age: 34 ★ **Position:** Defender

Lowdown: Just squeezing into the top 50, Short is a surprising selection. But his contribution should not be underestimated, as he used all his experience to ensure his club's safety despite being sent-off three times.

MATCHFACTS RATINGS		
PLAYED	STARS	AVERAGE
22	2	6.86

48

MATTHEW PIPER
Leicester City

Age: 21 ★ **Position:** Midfielder

Lowdown: Piper was a bright spark in a dire season for The Foxes, and his pace and trickery caused real problems for many top-class defenders. Mainly a right-winger, the young Leicester lad looks to have a bright future.

MATCHFACTS RATINGS		
PLAYED	STARS	AVERAGE
16	2	6.86

49

FREDDIE KANOUTE
West Ham United

Age: 25 ★ **Position:** Striker

Lowdown: A decent return of 11 Premiership goals from 27 games is no small achievement for Kanoute, especially as West Ham struggled for large parts of the 2001-02 season. The lively French striker has become an eye-catching all-round talent, combining his electric pace and quick feet with an ability to find the net from all sorts of angles.

MATCHFACTS RATINGS		
PLAYED	STARS	AVERAGE
27	5	6.85

50

ROBBIE FOWLER
Leeds United

Age: 27 ★ **Position:** Striker

Lowdown: Fed up with spending his time warming the Liverpool bench, Robbie Fowler moved to Leeds last November and scored 12 goals in 22 games to finish as top scorer at Elland Road. His good form also helped get him into England's World Cup squad – the main reason why he left Anfield. Robbie scored 15 goals in total last season - including three for Liverpool in ten games – which was his best overall tally since the 1996-97 campaign.

MATCHFACTS RATINGS		
PLAYED	STARS	AVERAGE
32	7	6.84

>FOOTY MAD!<

WE'VE GONE CAPTION CRAZY!
There's always room for a laugh at someone else's expense - as this selection of MATCH pics shows!

Poor old Dave seems to have been caught short!

Boro have never been able to replace Ravanelli, no matter how hard they try!

Steffen Iversen remembers he's missed Hoddle's bible meeting.

"No Tugay, just break his leg, that'll do son."

"Glenda? No-one's called me that before – that's a clever joke Coley son, well done!"

"Aargh, Mr Invisible is pulling on my damn hair again!"

Not that Charlton like to surrender or anything!

Boro fans follow Beni Carbone's shot all the way out of the stadium...

...and Ranieri thinks of signing him.

Mboma practises 'The Sunderland', a pose where you nearly score, but very rarely do.

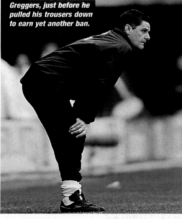

Greggers, just before he pulled his trousers down to earn yet another ban.

Den spots his mum in the crowd. Bless.

"Do I still get bum fluff? No, I shave like a man, for sure!"

Even after Peter Crouched, he still dwarfed the cameraman!

Jamo had to hit the bottle before his next trip to the hairdressers!

Ryan's new video, 'Let's Football Disco Dance', hits the stores this Christmas. It's a corker!

MATCH

RIVALDO Brazil

PERFECT MORNING?

"I'd get up about midday. I normally get up about 8.30am, so I'd have a lie-in for a change. Breakfast would be something like eggs, bacon and sausages. Normally it's all cereals, toast and healthier food, so I'd like to have a nice big fry-up for a change!"

PERFECT AFTERNOON?

"I'd go to the beach and relax! I'd just chill out with my friends on the beach and enjoy being in the sun. I wouldn't train because I'd need the rest! Don't get me wrong, I do like training, especially with the quality of players that Arsenal have. It used to be like, 'Ugh, I've got to get up early and go training', but with so many great players at the club now, I always enjoy it."

PERFECT DINNER?

"I'd just go out for something to eat with my friends, relax and have fun. I think I'd go for McDonalds. I don't mind going out to restaurants, but McDonalds is my favourite. Otherwise, I'd probably have a piece of fish or a steak."

PERFECT GAME?

"I probably wouldn't watch any football. I don't see much unless I'm watching Arsenal! I'll sometimes watch Man. United, but too much football can get a bit boring."

PERFECT EVENING?

"I wouldn't be out too late. I didn't go out much when I was young - I was too busy playing football. I've been football mad ever since I was a baby. I can't go out too much anyway now, but that's a sacrifice you have to make. I have to train every day and look after my body. I don't really go out much - I'm quite boring really and just watch TV!"

Ashley Cole's...
Perfect day!

Sunshine, fast cars and cool tunes! Arsenal & England star Ashley Cole tells MATCH how he'd spend his perfect 24 hours!

PERFECT MOTOR?

"That's tough because there's quite a big choice, but I suppose it would have to be a Ferrari. A convertible Ferrari in black!"

PERFECT TUNES?

"I'd be listening to a bit of r'n'b. It's nice chill-out music, isn't it? Ludacris is one I'd have on, and then Ja Rule and Sisqo. The Ja Rule album, 'Vinni Vetti Vecci' is one we always listen to at training. Before a game at Arsenal, we normally listen to something a bit more hyped up."

PERFECT PLACE?

"I think I'd spend my perfect day in California. I've never been out there on holiday before, but I've seen it on the television and it looks really nice!"

United won their fourth Premiership title in 1997.

fourth XI

The Premiership's only been around since the 1992-93 season, but what do you know about it?

1 It's been nearly ten years since it happened, but which team won the first ever Premiership title?

2 And who managed that side to their 1993 league triumph?

3 The Premiership's leading scorer is still going strong today, but what's his name?

4 And what famous landmark did that striker reach during the 2001-02 season?

5 Manchester United finished third in the Premiership last season. Why was that a first for them?

6 Back in 1996-97, Manchester United won the Premiership with the lowest points total ever. What was it?

7 Three teams are relegated from the Premiership every season, but who were the first three?

8 True or false? The very first sponsor of the Premiership was brewers Carling.

9 Which player holds the record for the fastest ever goal in the Premiership?

10 Which team did Manchester United beat 9-0 in the 1994-95 season?

11 Which team in the Premiership became the first ever to field a completely non-English XI for a league game?

1 POINT PER CORRECT ANSWER

BALL GAMES

Starting at No.1, fill in the answers (the last letter of each answer is the first letter of the next), complete the circle and re-arrange the yellow letters to reveal an Arsenal and France superstar.

1. The surname of Brazil's left-back Roberto.
2. Middlesbrough's World Cup centre-back.
3. This team plays at Goodison Park.
4. The big American city where the Metrostars play.
5. Republic Of Ireland winger, Kevin.
6. King Cantona's first name.

10 POINTS FOR CORRECT ANSWER

⚽ GAFFER FORCE ⚽

MATCH puts the World Cup managers in the spotlight!

Hi, my name's Gus Hiddink, but which 2002 World Cup team did I manage?

2 POINTS FOR CORRECT ANSWER

ONE OF A KIND

Cross out the letters appearing more than once and unscramble the leftovers to reveal the player.

T S R A N X C
S U B C I S T
X B X I E L T

3 POINTS FOR CORRECT ANSWER

ALAN SHEARER QUIZ

Big Al's loving life at Newcastle, but how much do you know about his career?

1 True or false? Shearer holds the record for the youngest player to score a league hat-trick.

2 Big Al scored on his England debut, but which country was it against?

3 How many goals did he score at Euro '96?

4 How much did Big Al cost Newcastle when he joined them in 1996?

5 And from which rival Premiership side did the striker join them from?

2 POINTS PER CORRECT ANSWER

anegrams

Rearrange the letters to find these World Cup stars!

1. HIM LEEK EYES
2. VIRTUOUS DANY LONER
3. A TRIVIA PICKER
4. ACHE PULL SOS
5. OK DRY WEIGHT

2 POINTS PER CORRECT ANSWER

WEIRD BEARDS

Try to identify these players just by looking at their facial fuzz.

3 POINTS PER CORRECT ANSWER

FREAK OR UNIQUE!

True or false? Peter Crouch has links with a family of giraffes.

2 POINTS FOR CORRECT ANSWER

74

MATCH

WORLD SUPERSTARS

MICHAEL OWEN England

PREMIERSHIP SUPER STRIKERS!

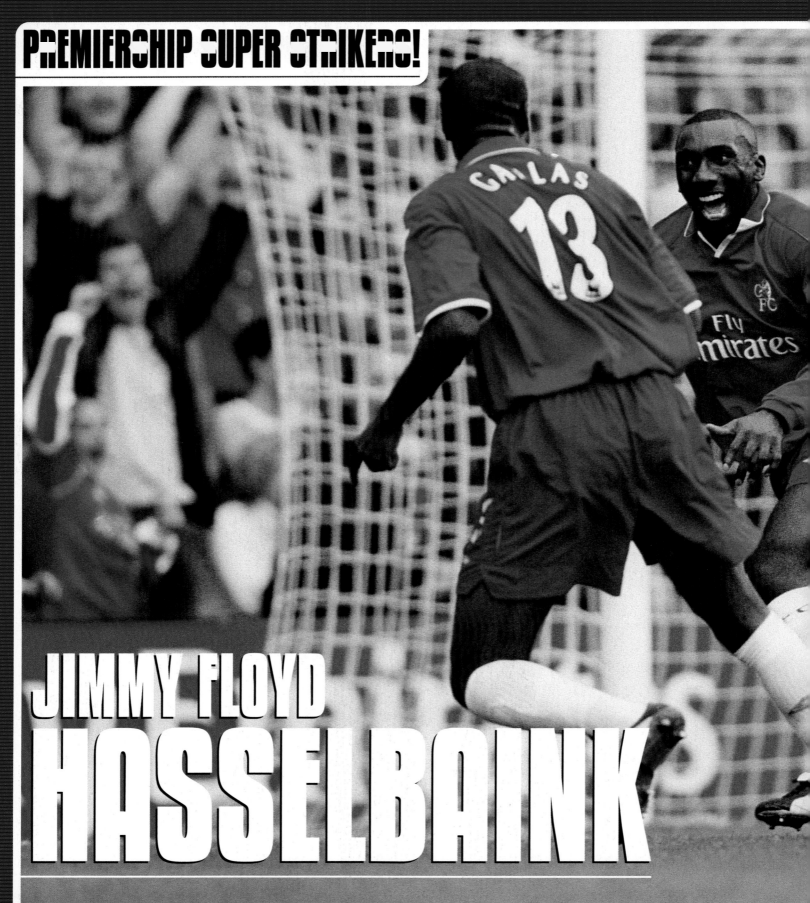

JIMMY FLOYD
HASSELBAINK

JIMMY FLOYD HASSELBAINK TIMELINE...

JUNE

MAKING A STAND
After leaving AZ Alkmaar, Jimmy refuses to sign forms with FC Zwolle, saying he couldn't afford to live with the terms they were offering.

1994

JUNE

PART-TIME PLAYER
Plays for amateur side Neerlinda in Holland as a striker for the first time and attracts attention from scouts and agents.

JUNE

PORTUGAL POWER
Makes a move to Campomairorense in Portugal, scoring 12 league goals in his first season.

1995

JULY

BOA BOY
Boavista snap him up and he scores 20 times in the league and helps the club lift the Portuguese Cup.

1996

JUNE

LEEDS LEAD THE WAY
With Europe's top clubs circling, George Graham brings the Dutchman to Elland Road for what he hopes will prove to be a bargain £2 million.

1997

MAY

TOP MAN
Top scores for Leeds with 22 goals – 16 in the Premiership.

1998

JUNE

WORLD CUP WONDER
Makes his debut at the World Cup finals, playing in the games against Belgium and Mexico.

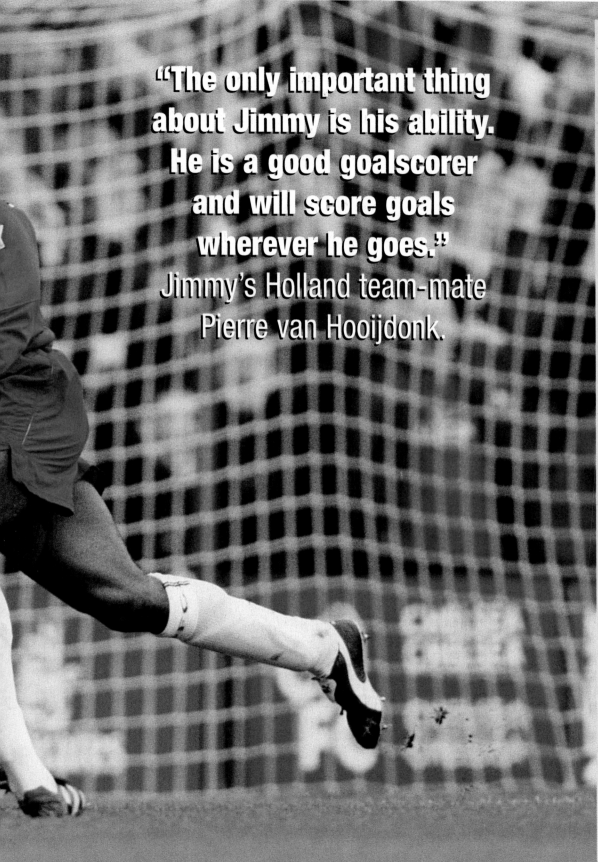

"The only important thing about Jimmy is his ability. He is a good goalscorer and will score goals wherever he goes."
Jimmy's Holland team-mate Pierre van Hooijdonk.

Jimmy's game is all about goals, but how did he become such a top striker?

Jimmy Floyd Hasselbaink is one of the Premiership's most deadly strikers, but he's had to work extremely hard to get where he is today. Jimmy was no child prodigy – in the end, his desire to get to the top made sure he did.

After failing to hit the big time in his home country of Holland, Jimmy moved to Portugal, where his career took off and his goal record with Campomairorense and Boavista earned him a big move to Leeds in 1997. He scored 34 league goals for the Yorkshire club in two seasons, before moving to Atletico Madrid for £12 million and scoring 24 goals in one season.

The Spaniards were forced to sell Jimmy in 2000, and Chelsea splashed out £15 million for him. But it's been money well spent, and in his first two seasons the hotshot striker notched 55 goals for The Blues. Quite simply, his goal record is the stuff of legends. And now MATCH can reveal the whole story behind Jimmy Floyd's rise to super striker status!

CAREER FACTFILE

Born:	March 27, 1972 in Paramaribo
Nationality:	Dutch
Position:	Striker
Height:	5ft 11ins
Weight:	13st 1lb
Former clubs:	Telstar, AZ Alkmaar, Neerlinda, Campomairorense, Boavista, Leeds, Atletico Madrid
Signed:	From Atletico Madrid for £15 million on June 2, 2000
Chelsea debut:	v Manchester United on August 13, 2000 (Charity Shield)
Total Chelsea games/goals:	89/55 (August 2000 to May 2002)
International caps/goals:	Holland 18/7 (March 1998 to July 2002)

CHART TOPPER
Top of the Leeds scoring charts again, bagging 18 Premiership goals.

1999

JUNE
LEAVES LEEDS
Leaves Elland Road after a contract dispute. Atletico Madrid pay £12 million.

MAY
PAIN IN SPAIN
Scoring 24 La Liga goals doesn't save Atletico from relegation.

JUNE
EURO OUT
Dropped from the Dutch squad for the Euro 2000 finals.

JULY
CHELSEA SMILE
Gianluca Vialli signs him for Chelsea for a record £15 million.

2000

AUGUST
NO CHARITY
Scores against Man. United as Chelsea win the Charity Shield.

HAMMER TIME
Finds the net against West Ham on his Chelsea Premiership debut.

OCTOBER
SENT TO COVENTRY
Bags four goals in a 6-1 rout over Coventry.

NOVEMBER
RED BULL
Red-carded after elbowing Everton's Michael Ball.

MAY
CITY SLICKER
Ends the season with a goal against Man. City, his 23rd.

2001

SEPTEMBER
WORLD CUP MISERY
Misses World Cup finals after Holland's 1-0 loss to Ireland.

RED CARD AGAIN
Sees red against Arsenal after a tussle with Keown.

DECEMBER
CHAMPS KO'D
Opens scoring at Old Trafford as Chelsea crush Man. United 3-0.

JANUARY
SPURS TOO HOT
Loses 5-1 to Spurs in the League Cup semi-final.

FEBRUARY
ENGLAND TEST
Plays for Holland against England but fails to score.

2002

APRIL
AT THE DOUBLE
Ends five-game league barren spell with a double against Everton.

MAY
CUP FINAL MISERY
Loses FA Cup final to Arsenal and is taken off in the second half.

1995

PORTUGAL PREDATOR

After spells in Holland with Telstar, AZ Alkmaar and Neerlinda, big Hasselbaink moved to modest club Campomairorense in Portugal. There his career took off, and he became known as 'Jimmy'.

You see, his real name's Jerrel, but the Campo chairman didn't want anyone to know the identity of the player he was trying to sign and told journalists he was called Jimmy. Under his new guise things went well. He scored 12 league goals in one season before netting 19 in 20 games for Boavista in the 1996-97 campaign.

1997

LEEDS LOVE JIMMY

Jimmy was still an unknown outside of Portugal, but Leeds manager George Graham had already seen enough of him to pay £2 million for the striker in the summer of 1997. The powerful star didn't waste any time at Elland Road, scoring on his debut against Arsenal and going on to net an impressive 22 times that season, with 16 coming in the Premiership alone.

His no-nonsense approach to scoring was a big hit with the Leeds fans and George Graham's modest outlay on the 26-year-old had already paid off. Jimmy had become a huge star, and defenders throughout the land feared facing the powerful striker.

"He's a real predator, his desire to find the net is unbelievable and he will do anything to score." Chelsea team-mate Eidur Gudjohnsen.

1998

WORLD CUP JOY

For a player who had never represented his country at any level before, Jimmy's sudden rise to fame in the national side looked complete when he was included in Holland's squad for the 1998 World Cup in France.

Having made his international debut against the Czech Republic in March, Jimmy started the first game for his country against Belgium in the finals before he came off for Dennis Bergkamp. He played one more time in the tournament, against Mexico, as the Dutch made it to the semis, where they lost to Brazil.

He was disappointed to only feature twice in the event, but the experience he gained would only serve to make him an even better striker in club football.

1999

ELLAND ROAD EXIT

Jimmy's 18 Premiership goals guided Leeds to fourth place in the 1998-99 season, which also earned the club a lucrative place in the UEFA Cup. His status as one of the club's most prolific strikers ever was now assured, having racked up 34 league goals in just 66 starts. The Elland Road faithful loved him, but it would soon turn very sour in West Yorkshire.

Jimmy, armed with his impressive goals-to-games-ratio, went to chairman Peter Ridsdale asking for an improved contract. He felt the deal offered wasn't suitable, and the club promptly sold him to Spanish club Atletico Madrid for £12 million. The English Press labelled Jimmy as greedy and the fans turned just as quickly, but the player himself still looks back on his time at Leeds as the pivotal years in his career.

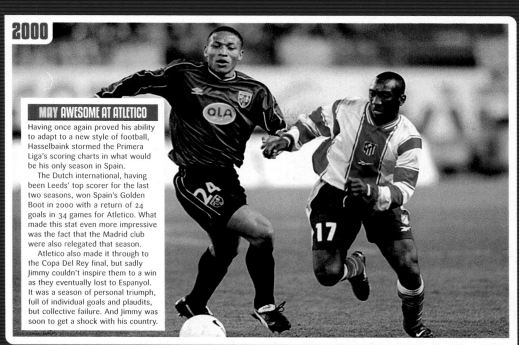

2000

MAY AWESOME AT ATLETICO

Having once again proved his ability to adapt to a new style of football, Hasselbaink stormed the Primera Liga's scoring charts in what would be his only season in Spain.

The Dutch international, having been Leeds' top scorer for the last two seasons, won Spain's Golden Boot in 2000 with a return of 24 goals in 34 games for Atletico. What made this stat even more impressive was the fact that the Madrid club were also relegated that season.

Atletico also made it through to the Copa Del Rey final, but sadly Jimmy couldn't inspire them to a win as they eventually lost to Espanyol. It was a season of personal triumph, full of individual goals and plaudits, but collective failure. And Jimmy was soon to get a shock with his country.

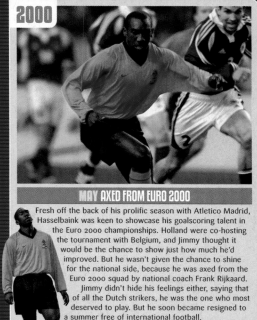

2000

MAY AXED FROM EURO 2000

Fresh off the back of his prolific season with Atletico Madrid, Hasselbaink was keen to showcase his goalscoring talent in the Euro 2000 championships. Holland were co-hosting the tournament with Belgium, and Jimmy thought it would be the chance to show just how much he'd improved. But he wasn't given the chance to shine for the national side, because he was axed from the Euro 2000 squad by national coach Frank Rijkaard. Jimmy didn't hide his feelings either, saying that of all the Dutch strikers, he was the one who most deserved to play. But he soon became resigned to a summer free of international football.

2000

JULY CHELSEA'S MULTI-MILLION SWOOP

Despite all the goals he'd scored in Spain, Atletico were in huge debt after relegation from La Liga and had to cash in their prized asset. With the likes of Lazio, Real Madrid, Valencia and Tottenham in the hunt for him, Jimmy decided to return to the Premiership with Chelsea – the club who had tried to sign him the year before.

Boss Gianluca Vialli convinced the club to pay the £15 million asking price and make him their record transfer. Vialli was sure the Dutchman with the scoring touch was the final piece in his jigsaw, and the man to score the goals Chelsea had often lacked.

2001

GOLDEN BOOT WINNER

The simple fact is that strikers are paid to score goals, and in the 2000-2001 season Jimmy earned every penny of his huge salary at Stamford Bridge. He netted on his debut for the club, in the Charity Shield against Man. United, and ended the season as the Premiership's top scorer with 23 strikes.

Personal highlights included a four-goal blast against Coventry City, a brace in the 2-2 draw at Liverpool, and goals in both the league games against Man. United. Despite the team playing below par, and Vialli being replaced by Claudio Ranieri early on, the one thing you could be sure of was JFH's ability to find the net.

2002

MAY GOAL CRAZY

Jimmy's goal statistics already made impressive reading – but after the 2001-2002 season they ranked with the best in the Premiership. That season Hasselbaink fired in another 23 league goals for Chelsea, one behind Golden Boot winner Thierry Henry, to bring his account for the club to 46 goals in 70 league games.

But looking back over his four years in England, Jimmy's record makes even better reading! Up to the summer of 2002, he'd played in 176 competitive games for Chelsea and Leeds, scoring 97 goals along the way. That adds up to more than a one-in-two strike rate. Get in!

2002

MAY FA CUP FINAL LOSER

While Hasselbaink's time in England has mainly been full of highs, he's still yet to win a major trophy in this country and it's clearly something that bugs the super striker. In interviews with MATCH, he's always told us he'd swap all his goals for a winners' medal.

Sadly, Jimmy was left empty-handed again in 2002, as Chelsea finished fifth in the league and lost the FA Cup final to Arsenal. He scored in the fourth and fifth round against West Ham and Preston, but despite shaking off a calf injury to start the showcase final against Arsenal, he lasted just 68 minutes before being replaced as The Gunners won 2-0.

It was a sad end to the season for the Dutchman, but he'll be hoping that a winners' medal will eventually come his way at Chelsea.

MYSTIC MATCHMAN!

Matchy rubs his old crystal ball and predicts the footy future!

Alright, folks? Mystic MATCHMAN here – the foreseer of footy future, clairvoyant of classy calcio, and psychic of the soccer world! I see all and know all – well, I'm a know-all, but that's anuvver matter! To bring yer into the know about wot's gonna be goin' on in the footy world in the 2003-04 season, I've looked into me size five crystal ball and found out wot will 'appen. Welcome to the future…

AUGUST 2003
It sez in me crystal ball that Bolton will win the Charity Shield, beating Newcastle 3-2. In the Premiership, Arsenal's new £70 million signing Ronaldo cracks five goals past newly-promoted Grimsby, while Sven Goran Eriksson tells us that he'll jack in the England job after Euro 2004.

SEPTEMBER 2003
New Man. United gaffer Steve Bruce is well stressed after not recording a win since the beginning of the season, while table-toppers Man. City are flying in the Champions League. Roy Keane falls out with Stevie Bruce, tellin' him where he can stick his job. Sven resigns from the England job after grief from the Press. Dave Becks tops the pop charts with his debut single.

OCTOBER 2003
Pace-setters Celtic lead Division One by miles, but cash-strapped Chelsea are strugglin'. Steve Bruce walks out on Man. United to take up the manager's job at Leeds United, while Liverpool announce the signing of Roy Keane on a free from United. Man. United announce that Eric Cantona's their new gaffer. while FIFA announce that the 2010 World Cup will be held in Poland!

NOVEMBER 2003
Kevin Keegan is re-appointed England gaffer, sayin' that this time it'll be well good. Chelsea flog off all their foreign duffers to lower the wage bill and sign Dean Windass, Shaun Goater and Keith Curle on free transfers. Ronaldo smashes his 30th of the season for Arsenal against Blackburn, and Steve Bruce sez he's leaving Leeds to take up the gaffer's job at Everton.

> MATCHMAN told me I'd join Arsenal!

DECEMBER 2003
Cantona makes Luke Chadwick his new captain at Man. United. Stevie McManaman and Robbie Fowler, together again at Everton, help The Toffees knock Liverpool out of the FA Cup. Phil Thompson and Gerard Houllier, The Reds' gaffers, jack it in. Robbie Savage wins Sports Personality Of The Year 2003!

JANUARY 2004
A start of anuvver year, and Steve Bruce takes up the Liverpool manager's post after walking out on Everton. Ronaldo scores his 40th of the season for Arsenal. Bobby Robson signs a new contract at Newcastle, keeping him at the club until he's 120, while Dave Becks receives a knighthood.

FEBRUARY 2004
Keegan recalls Dennis Wise and sticks Gareth Southgate into midfield for his first England friendly in charge, but they lose 2-0 to Malta. New Chelsea gaffer Dave Bassett takes Chelsea into the Division One play-offs, while Ronaldo nets his 50th bloomin' goal of the season!

MARCH 2004
Liverpool's Michael Owen is sold to Inter Milan for £58 million by Steve Bruce, who says it woz too good an offer to turn down. Cheltenham win the League Cup final wiv a 1-0 win over Blackpool at Shrewsbury's Gay Meadow.

APRIL 2004
The Premiership's hotting up nicely, wiv Man. City and Newcastle vying for top spot. Steve Bruce leaves Liverpool after the fans call for his head. Eric Cantona is under pressure at Man. United after it's revealed that he makes his players train in a cage. Celtic win promotion to the Premiership without breaking sweat.

MAY 2004
Newcastle take the Premiership title for the second season running. Sir Bobby Robson is given anuvver knighthood, making him Sir Sir Bobby Robson. Stevie Bruce rejoins Man. United in time to win the FA Cup with a 2-0 win over Glasgow Rangers. Ronaldo hits his 60th of the season, but misses out on the Golden Boot to Palace's 64-goal Ade Akinbiyi. Dave Bassett's Chelsea win promotion to the Premiership. As for me, well that's me bizness, innit? See ya!

"You can… quote me on that"

"Germany are a very difficult team to play. They had 11 internationals out there today."
Northern Ireland international Steve Lomas explains just how good Northern Ireland's opponents really are!

"I definitely want Brooklyn to be christened, but I don't know into what religion yet."
David Beckham gets a little bit confused again. We wonder if he celebrates Christmas?

"The Brazilians were South American, and the Ukrainians are sure to be more European."
Phil Neville gives his expert analysis to a series of friendlies England have to play.

"One accusation you can't throw at me is that I've always done my best."
Alan Shearer – one of the least dedicated players in English football, or so the legendary striker claims!

"Sometimes in football you have to score goals."
That's what Arsenal's super striker Thierry Henry reckons. Wise words from the French star, don't you reckon?

"Second best is not good enough really. Although if someone turned around now and said, 'You will be promoted, but you will come in second', then I would take it."
So says Man. City defender Steve Howey – a man who knows what he wants!

"He can't head the ball, tackle, or kick with his left foot. And he doesn't score enough goals."
Man. United legend George Best gives his expert opinion on England skipper David Beckham. So apart from all that, he's pretty good at this footy lark, eh Bestie?

MATCH

THIERRY HENRY France

ME! LOOKING WELL SMART :-)

GIGGS: MY

Ryan Giggs is a legend at Manchester United. At a club with a truckload of stars, the flying winger has managed to stand out for over a decade as one of the most exciting players of his generation. The likes of Eric Cantona, Peter Schmeichel, Paul Ince, Mark Hughes and Andy Cole have been and gone at Old Trafford, but Giggs has been a permanent fixture in the team for well over ten years.

Giggs first appeared for United towards the end of the 1990-91 season, when the Alex Ferguson era was beginning to take off. Seasons on, Ryan's still doing what he does best, tormenting defenders all over Europe. His personal trophy cabinet is bulging at the seams, with medals from countless Premier League triumphs, FA Cup wins and the famous European Cup victory in 1999, and he hasn't finished yet.

"It feels like it's gone quickly when you look at the old pictures and clippings of yourself from ten years of playing in the first team," Giggs told us. **"You take it in stages. The first is to get in the team and the next is to stay there. I've just been lucky that I've been here in an era when United have won so much."**

MATCH has never been far away from Giggs, from his United debut to the present day. Now, with help from man himself, it's time to open up the Giggsy scrapbook to recall his most memorable moments!

▲ IT'S A DREAM START FOR YOUNG RYAN

Giggs couldn't have got off to a much better start at United. In March 1991 he made his senior debut as a sub against Everton at Old Trafford. A short while later, the 17-year-old was on from the start for a biggie – against Man. City – and scored the only goal in a 1-0 win. Officially, anyway. **"This was an own goal but I claimed it anyway,"** he said. **"It was my first Manchester derby in front of 45,000 at Old Trafford and it was amazing. To score the winner in such a massive game at 17 was an unbelievable feeling and it doesn't matter to me that it wasn't my goal – the history books will say I scored and that's what matters!"**

SCRAPBOOK!

YOU CAN SHAKE A STICK AT — HERE'S GIGGSY'S LIFE IN WORDS AND PICTURES!

◄ THE WELSH WIZARD

Giggsy had only just started his professional career when his first international call-up came knocking. By coming on as an 86th-minute substitute for Wales against West Germany on October 16, 1991, Ryan became the youngest-ever player to represent his country. For the record, Wales lost the match 4-1, but Giggsy was just 17 years old at the time. His first international start was a little longer in coming, but more successful. On March 31, 1993 he scored with an outstanding free-kick as Wales beat Belgium in Cardiff – the city of his birth.

◄ PLAYER OF THE YEAR

With his dazzling wing play and wicked footwork, it wasn't long before Ryan really caught the eye. The fans loved him, and so did the other players – so much so that Giggs was voted PFA Young Player Of The Year two years in succession by his fellow pros! In 1992, he lined up before the photographers with United team-mate Gary Pallister, who was named Player Of The Year. It was same again in 1993, but this time with former Old Trafford icon Paul McGrath. Giggs had quickly become the most exciting young player in the country, bar none.

▲ LEAGUE CUP KINGS

As a newcomer in the side, Ryan watched United upset Barcelona to win the European Cup Winners' Cup in 1991. He wasn't involved on the night, but a year later he was in the team which lifted the 1992 League Cup, beating Nottingham Forest. It was Ryan's first major cup final with United: **"In the league we missed out at the death, so it was good we won this trophy. I'd played at Wembley before, but this was my first time for the senior side in a cup final and it was fantastic. I set up the winner for Brian McClair in a 1-0 win and really enjoyed it."**

"Please Mr Giggs, can I have your autograph?" Ryan has always found time to please his many fans with a personal signature!

◄ IT'S GIGGS MANIA! ►

By 1993, Ryan was well established as one of the game's leading lights. His electric pace and exciting style made him an obvious hero, and his good looks marked him out as the perfect role model. He signed a big sponsorship deal with Reebok and suddenly everyone wanted a piece of him – Giggsy became an overnight sensation! **"You're just leaving school and then you're playing football the next year in the first team and you just want to enjoy it,"** he recalled. **"But then the next minute the Press are camping outside your house and want to know all about your family, your background, your girlfriend – I think for me that was the hardest thing to have to cope with."** The young superstar knew that he would have to learn how to handle his new-found fame quickly.

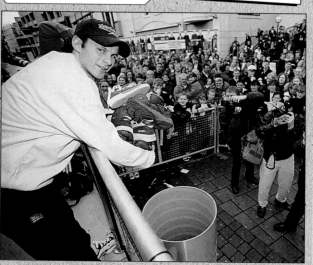

By 1997 Giggs was an old hand at taking part in ads and commercials, but being transformed into an evil cartoon character was a completely new experience, even for him. The 'Doppelganger' ad, shot for Reebok, featured a good Giggs being captured and replaced by a villainous version who played for arch rivals Man. City and was intent on causing chaos! **"I never thought the result would be this good,"** said an impressed Ryan after seeing the short film. **"The puppet sculptors have done a great job in making the models look like the real thing. They say that everyone has a double, but if mine's anything like the one in the film I hope I never meet him!"** By the way, it all turned out well in the end. Good Giggsy escaped and arrived just in time to save the day, scoring past a monster goalie!

▲ READING WITH ROBBO

Giggsy's always loved MATCH. Here he is in 1993 reading the magazine with United legend Bryan Robson!

▲ CHAMPIONSHIP GLORY ARRIVES – AT LONG LAST!

The lengthy period of time without a league championship had been a millstone around the necks of all United fans, players and managers for 26 years, and it felt worse after the narrow failure in 1992. But the year after it was glory, glory Man. United as The Red Devils won the title for the first time since the '60s. Giggs was delighted and relieved! **"I'll always remember the relief. We were thinking, 'Are we ever going to win the league?' because it had been such a long time. It was a joke for United not to have won the league for so long, so it was a relief. You could see it in the players' faces, you could see it in the fans, so that was probably one of the memories that will stick with me."**

Hi-tech trickery is used to produce a 1994 TV ad with Ryan alongside George Best and Bobby Charlton in United's greatest team.

KING ERIC'S REIGN ▶

A major reason for United's domestic success in the '90s was the influence of French ace Eric Cantona. Giggs was a big fan: **"When I think about Eric I think about the cup final goal against Liverpool in 1996. It's him all over, coming up with the goods at the right time. It was a big game and a goal only he'd have scored."**

DOING THE DOUBLE ▶

Once United got going, they took a lot of stopping, and in the 1993-94 season no-one was able to do it. Giggsy and his team-mates beat all comers to win the coveted 'double' of championship title and FA Cup. In the league, United triumphed over Blackburn Rovers by an eight-point margin, while in the FA Cup final, Chelsea were easily swept aside 4-0. A brilliant team was in the making. **"To win the league two years on the trot takes a lot, so that was great,"** said Giggs. **"We had a great side that year and we played really well and deserved to win the title again. We were still on a high from the league when we came down to Wembley to play in the FA Cup final. No Man. United side had ever won two trophies in one season, so that was a big incentive for us."**

SIGN LANGUAGE ▶

"It doesn't take much to give up a bit of your time to sign autographs and after all, where would we be without the fans?"

THE MODEL PRO ▶

Between all the winning of trophies, there was always time for fun off the pitch, and at times the photoshoots came thick and fast. In this 1996 shoot, Giggsy indulged in a spot of fashion modelling for his sponsors, Reebok. "I don't mind doing things like this because I love checking out clothes," he told MATCH at the time. "When Paul Ince was at the club he used to slaughter me if I wasn't dressed up in the latest designer gear, but he can't do that to me any more, can he?" Er, don't bet on that one, Ryan!

When Giggsy isn't ripping up defences he's posing for his fave footy magazine. Here he is in casual gear, perched on a wall!

◀ TAKE THAT, BARÇA!

Giggs revelled in the class opposition United faced during their memorable 1998-99 Champions League run. Playing against the best in Europe inspired top performances from him, and it seemed the bigger the team, the better Giggsy got. He opened the scoring against Barcelona in a thrilling group game which finished 3-3 in September 1998. "I've always enjoyed the big games," said Ryan. "It's why you become a footballer, you want to play in the big games as much as you can – Barcelona, Inter Milan and so on. I love being part of games like that."

"I used to play a lot of basketball, not just in the playground but against other schools. I used to really enjoy doing that."

JUVE BEEN GIGGS-IED! ▶

Confirming his reputation as a big-game player, Ryan popped up with a vital strike in the semi-finals of the 1999 Champions League. Juventus were within seconds of leaving Old Trafford with a victory when Giggs thundered home an equaliser. It set up a classic second leg, which United won 3-2 to reach the final.

◀ THE GOLDEN GOAL

It wouldn't be difficult to pick a top ten selection of Ryan's best goals and each one would be real quality, but one stands head and shoulders above the rest. In April 1999, in the FA Cup semi-final replay against Arsenal, the scores were level at 1-1 going into extra-time. United were without Roy Keane, who had been sent-off, and The Gunners were favourites to win – until Giggsy jinked past Arsenal's defence for a stunning winner. "This is the best goal I've ever scored," he said. "We weren't favourites playing extra-time with ten men so when I scored it was an amazing feeling. I was pleased with the goal, but the way the match was set up really added to it. It's great to score a goal in a big game, the semi-final of the FA Cup, when the team really needs it."

GIGGSY'S Big moments!

SEPTEMBER 1993

On September 19, Giggs was in the side which beat Arsenal 1-0 at Old Trafford, and that crucial win set the team off on an amazing unbeaten run. Man. United didn't lose another league game until March 5, 1994, when they lost 1-0 away to Chelsea!

NOVEMBER 1993

As United chased European glory, there was an ugly welcome for Giggs and his team-mates in Turkey. The team touched down at Istanbul airport to be greeted with taunting banners proclaiming, 'Welcome To Hell' from Galatasaray fans. United drew the game 0-0 and went out on away goals.

MARCH 1994

United made it through to the League Cup final, but they were beaten by Aston Villa. Former Red Devils boss Ron Atkinson guided his Villa side to a 3-1 win and the chance of winning a trio of domestic trophies was lost.

MAY 1994

This was a great month for United. The club retained the league title and then overwhelmed Chelsea 4-0 in the FA Cup final to win the coveted double for the first time. Giggs hit 17 goals in all domestic competitions.

SEPTEMBER 1994

United's surprise 3-2 defeat at Ipswich Town had far-reaching consequences for Giggs. He injured himself during the game, and after that his form wasn't that good. In fact, he scored just one league goal during the whole of the campaign.

MAY 1995

The season ended pretty miserably for United. A 1-1 draw at West Ham allowed the title to go to Blackburn instead, but Giggs didn't even play as he missed the last six league games due to injury. And in the FA Cup final, Everton shocked United by winning 1-0. Ryan was only fit enough to replace Steve Bruce as a substitute.

AUGUST 1995

A new-look United started the 1995-96 season. Andrei Kanchelskis, Paul Ince and Mark Hughes were all sold in the summer and Alex Ferguson put his faith instead in young stars such as David Beckham, Nicky Butt and Gary Neville. But a defeat away to Aston Villa on the opening day had the critics predicting a bad season.

SEPTEMBER 1995

United's European campaign didn't last long. The side, playing in the UEFA Cup, went out in the first round to little-known side Rotor Volgograd on away goals – despite a late goal from goalkeeper Peter Schmeichel at Old Trafford! The season was barely a month old and already the team had been rocked by disappointment.

OCTOBER 1995

There was further embarrassment for Giggs and United as the team crashed out of the League Cup to York City. Giggs played in both legs as the Division Two side recorded a 3-0 win at Old Trafford and went through despite losing the second leg 3-1.

MAY 1996

Having put their early season troubles behind them, Man. United finished the season on top and Giggs again played a major part. His tally of 11 league goals pushed The Red Devils to yet another league title, while in the FA Cup final, Liverpool were beaten 1-0 thanks to an Eric Cantona special. The French master volleyed a late winner to seal a great triumph.

APRIL 1997

Heartbreak for United. After beating Porto 4-0 in the quarter-finals – Giggs scored one of the goals – the team were knocked out in the semi-finals by Borussia Dortmund. And Ryan was left out of the team for the second leg, as Fergie decided to play Ole Gunnar Solskjaer. At least another title was sealed, but the big trophy still eluded Ryan and his team-mates.

CHAMPIONS OF EUROPE - AND TREBLE WINNERS ▶

With the league title and FA Cup in the bag, United stood on the verge of an historic 'treble' when they faced Bundesliga side Bayern Munich in the final of the 1999 Champions League. Munich took an early lead through Mario Basler and all seemed lost as the game drifted into injury-time. But Teddy Sheringham grabbed an equaliser and then, with the Germans fading fast, Ole Gunnar Solskjaer poached a dramatic winner. It was a fantastic night, and capped Ryan's most memorable season. **"The European Cup final has been my best moment,"** he said. **"Winning the league for the first time with United was unbelievable, but the next step was Europe and we had come so close before. Even now I look back on that game and still find it difficult to believe what actually happened. It wasn't just a normal game and it wasn't just a normal night. I guess for the first time we had ridden our luck and luck had favoured us. To create history by winning three competitions is an incredible feat, and no one will ever be able to take that way from us."**

Good luck Giggsy! United fans line up to wish the players all the best before the classic 1999 Champions League final v Bayern Munich.

▲ UNITED MOTOR ON!

There was an added bonus for Ryan right at the end of 1999. He helped United become the first British team to win the World Club Championship in Tokyo, beating Palmeiras 1-0 with a Roy Keane goal. He was also given a brand new car from cup sponsors Toyota as a prize for being named Man Of The Match! Get in Giggsy!

Giggsy's gonna get ya! Ryan takes aim and fires as he helps to launch a new boot for sponsors Reebok. It's a scary sight for defenders!

▲ THE BOSS AND ME

From skinny-legged youngster to established first-team star, Ryan has always been able to turn to one man for valuable advice at any time – Sir Alex Ferguson. Like so many other United players who have come through the ranks at Old Trafford, Giggs has always enjoyed a great relationship with the gaffer over the years. **"The boss signed me for United as a young lad when I was 14 years old, and ever since then he's been brilliant to me,"** said Ryan. **"He's always given me good advice and not just about things on the pitch. He's always said to me: 'If you've got problems with your football, come and talk to me, the door is always open'. That's something I've used throughout my United career and I've found it's always helped me."**

UNITED v THE WORLD ▶

Instead of opening the year 2000 with an FA Cup tie, United travelled all the way over to Brazil for the Club World Championship, an eight-team tournament designed to find the best club side on the entire planet. United 'opted out' of the FA Cup to take part and before flying to Rio, Giggsy admitted he was looking forward to the challenge. **"It would be a great title to have – world champions. It's going to be a great tournament, where you're playing the very best teams in the world. We all want new challenges, and after winning the European Cup, the next step is to become world champions. To do that we have to overcome the South American teams and hopefully we can do that."** It didn't work out though, as United bowed out in the group stage.

JUST A BIG KID ▶

It's Giggs United! Ryan with just some of the fans hoping to follow in his footsteps at Old Trafford one day.

▲ EURO CROWN SLIPS

Defending the Champions League in 2000, United looked good for a repeat, but quarter-final opponents Real Madrid posed a stern test. After drawing 0-0 in Spain, United were favourites but lost 3-2 at Old Trafford, with Roy Keane scoring an own goal. Defeat was hard to take. "We didn't perform out in Madrid. We didn't reach the standards we'd set over the last few years, where we'd been to Milan and Juventus and scored goals. We had a really good chance, because all we had to do was win at home, but we knew we didn't have an away goal."

GIVE US A HUG BECKS ▶

Putting the disappointment of the Champions League failure behind them, United made up for it in the usual way by coasting to another league championship success. They finished top of the Premiership with 91 points; nearest rivals Arsenal only had 73 in comparison. It was easy. "After doing so well in 1999 in the Champions League, it was a bit of a letdown, but it was always going to be difficult to follow that treble-winning year," said Ryan. "We did run away with the Premiership title though, and I don't think you should ever underestimate what a fine achievement it is to win your own league. Even though we've won it many times in recent years, it's still a very tough championship to win. I never get tired of lifting trophies, anyway!"

In the summer of 2001, Giggsy and MATCH link up again, this time to produce a super CD-ROM full of his best tricks and top info!

▲ BACKING EURO 2000

Sadly for Ryan, Wales didn't qualify to take part in the 2000 European Championships, but that didn't stop our mate happily backing MATCH's magazine – published especially to preview the tournament in Holland and Belgium. Before he jetted off for some holiday time, Giggsy gave the mag the thumbs-up. Good on ya!

Caught red-handed! Giggs makes hand and foot prints in paint to raise the profile of a UNICEF campaign in April 2002.

RYAN GIGGS: MATCHMAN OF THE YEAR 2001 ▲

Of course, since Ryan emerged on the scene as a precocious talent in 1991, the UK's biggest and best footy magazine has been with him every step of the way. So it was fitting that ten years after breaking into the Man. United first team, Giggsy was revealed as the 2001 MATCHMAN Of The Season – his consistent performances edging him ahead of Roy Keane, Joe Cole, Paolo Di Canio and Sol Campbell at the top of the pile. "I was delighted," said Giggs. "I've had a long association with MATCH, and it's a very important magazine for football fans, so it's great news for me to come out on top. To finish as the best player in the Premiership over 38 league games is brilliant."

GIGGSY'S Big moments!

FEBRUARY 1998

Disaster for Giggs. He scored the first goal in a 2-0 success over Derby at Pride Park, but picked up a nasty hamstring injury which took time to clear up. He missed some crucial matches, not least the home clash against Arsenal – which United lost – and the European Cup quarter-final defeat to Monaco. The title slipped away and went to Highbury instead.

APRIL 1999

Giggsy scored possibly the goal of his life against Arsenal in the FA Cup semi-final replay at Villa Park. After a dull first game ended 0-0, the replay exploded into life. With the score at 1-1 – Arsenal had just missed a Dennis Bergkamp penalty and United were down to ten men after Roy Keane's dismissal – Giggs struck. In extra-time he got the ball just inside the Arsenal half and weaved his way past several challenges before beating David Seaman with a stunning strike.

MAY 1999

United sealed a remarkable treble success with three big trophies – the Premiership championship, FA Cup and European Cup. Giggs was in the team which beat Newcastle United at Wembley to lift the FA Cup, then again four days later as Man. United beat Bayern Munich 2-1 in Barcelona. The European triumph was amazing, with the English side coming from behind to win with two injury-time goals. The only disappointing aspect in an otherwise brilliant season for Ryan was his fitness – injuries limited his Premiership starts to just 20.

NOVEMBER 1999

Giggs broke new ground with United as the club won the FIFA World Club Championship by beating Palmeiras in the Toyota Cup. Captain Roy Keane scored the only goal of the game to seal a notable success. The memorable victory made United the first British team to win the cup, and Giggs was given a new car by the sponsors for being Man Of The Match!

JANUARY 2000

Ryan travelled out to Rio de Janeiro in Brazil for the first ever Club World Championship, but United played poorly. The team lost to Vasco da Gama, drew with Necaxa and then beat South Melbourne but failed to qualify for the next stage. And for that, United had forfeited the right to defend their FA Cup title.

APRIL 2000

Another league title success was achieved when United won 3-1 at Southampton. There were still four games remaining in the season when the triumph was sealed, but in the Champions League, United lost out to Real Madrid in the quarter-finals.

FEBRUARY 2001

In the Manchester United official club magazine, Giggs finished third in a poll to find the team's greatest player of all time. Eric Cantona won, George Best came second, then Ryan, with Bobby Charlton fourth in the voting.

APRIL 2001

Another season, another league championship. United again won at a canter and wrapped it up on April 14 against Coventry to make it three titles on the bounce. Giggs scored one of the goals in the 4-2 win – it was United's seventh title in nine seasons.

SEPTEMBER 2001

Ryan was sent-off for the first time in his career during Wales' international match in Norway. The Welsh lost the game, a World Cup qualifier, 3-2 and Giggs was dismissed five minutes from time for his second bookable offence. He was the captain, too.

MAY 2002

United lost the title when Arsenal beat them 1-0 at Old Trafford to claim the championship themselves. But the season finished on a better note for Ryan, as he played in the Wales team which beat Germany 1-0 in Cardiff.

87

>BIG MATCH QUIZ!<

Arsenal at the Double!

fifth XI

Arsenal won the Double in 2001-02, but how much can you remember from their victorious campaign?

1 How many points clear were Arsenal from second-placed Liverpool – a) three, b) five or c) seven?

2 Who finished top scorer for the Highbury club with 24 Premiership goals?

3 True or False? Arsenal's biggest away win was on the opening day against Middlesbrough.

4 How many 'keepers did The Gunners use in the Premiership?

5 Did Arsene Wenger's men draw the lucky north dressing room or the unlucky south dressing room for the FA Cup final against Chelsea?

6 Who scored The Gunners' first goal in the FA Cup final?

7 And who made it 2-0 in the 80th minute to send the red half of the Millennium Stadium crazy?

8 How many goals did Robert Pires score in the Premiership – a) seven, b) nine or c) eleven?

9 True or False? The Gunners beat Man. United home and away last season.

10 Which striker scored at Old Trafford to give Arsenal a 1-0 win and the title?

11 In which year did The Gunners first do the Double under Arsene Wenger?

1 POINT PER CORRECT ANSWER

GROUND FORCE

See if you can identify this Premiership ground.

1 POINT FOR CORRECT ANSWER

ONE OF A KIND

Cross out all the letters which turn up more than once, and unscramble the leftovers to reveal the mystery player.

W E U A T R O
Q N R D U P I
P O T R Q W Z

▢ ▢ ▢ ▢ ▢ ▢

2 POINTS FOR CORRECT ANSWER

LEGS ELEVEN

Which top players do these two lovely pairs of footballing pins belong to?

2 POINTS PER CORRECT ANSWER

FREAK OR UNIQUE!

True or false? Patrick Vieira needed a tongue transplant after a clash of heads while at former club AC Milan?

2 POINTS FOR CORRECT ANSWER

SAY WHAT?

Who is ex-England gaffer Glenn Hoddle talking about here?

I don't think he's a natural goalscorer.

2 POINTS FOR CORRECT ANSWER

WORD SEARCH

Try to pick out these England legends, who've all starred at international level for The Three Lions.

```
X P G W S N I K L I W W S N F M N U D
S K A D A M S H U N T S N Z Z A A F Q
U T N E J V Y B C R G T S R E T E P B
D G A G F A W X C J T D S Q P T Q Q C
E F P W H O D D L E B G E W G H X V A
H U R S T B A L L G R G L A A E R A N
W T G R E A V E S M O E O D S W Q O O
S E A M A N P Z B D O R H D C S T O T
W R I G H T Q V A L K R C L O L B H L
B A N K S F V Y R I I A S E I N O Q R
H L B V P O W W N N N R F H G O F Y A
O W E N I G W A E E G D S U N S E E H
H P K E E G A N S K P C R M E L R L C
S H E A R E R I E E K E O K S I D S N
R O B S O N A N C R H O A H F W I D N
S T I L E S M Z P C R G N R E Q N R H
P L A T T J L T T E Q Q O I C N A A S
B E C K H A M U B C B H E A Q E N E J
Q V Z N B D B J C A M P B E L L D B E
```

> Adams
> Ball
> Banks
> Barnes
> Beardsley
> Beckham
> Brooking
> Butcher
> Campbell
> Charlton
> Cohen
> Ferdinand
> Gascoigne
> Gerrard
> Greaves
> Hoddle
> Hunt
> Hurst
> Keegan
> Lineker
> Matthews
> Moore
> Owen
> Pearce
> Peters
> Platt
> Robson
> Scholes
> Seaman
> Shearer
> Shilton
> Stiles
> Waddle
> Wilkins
> Wilson
> Wright

1 POINT FOR CORRECT ANSWER (MAXIMUM 36 POINTS)

WHO AM I?

Which Newcastle star is being robbed here by Michael Carrick?

2 POINTS FOR CORRECT ANSWER

WORLD SUPERSTARS

FRANCESCO TOTTI Italy

>FINAL WHISTLE!<

61

Trailing 2-1 v Greece, your injury-time goal sends England to the World Cup!
Move to square 66

62

63

64

Noooo! You've broken a metatarsal bone in your left foot and are in danger of missing the World Cup!
Go back to square 55

65

60

59

58

57

You lead the England lads to an historic 5-1 win in Germany!
Move to square 63

56

41

42

43

Germany beat you in the last game at Wembley and the gaffer quits
Go back to square 37

44

45

40

39

...but you lose 3-2 and as you leave the pitch, some sick fans say nasty things about your wife and kid.
Go back to square 32

38

You play at Euro 2000 and set up two goals against Portugal...
Move to square 40

37

36

21

22

23

24

25

20

19

Nice one! England make it to the 1998 World Cup finals and you're in the squad!
Move to square 25

18

17

16

START
Are you up to being England skipper?
Let's see!

2

3

4

You make your full England debut in a tricky World Cup qualifier in Moldova!
Move to square 16

5

66

67
You score a penalty winner to beat Argentina. You're a national hero!
Move to the finish

68

69

FINISH
You're an England legend!

55

54

53

52
Ooooh, dodgy! You shave your hair into a mohican. That's no way for a captain to behave!
Go back to square 48

51

46

47
Great news! The new boss is Swedish and he makes you his captain!
Have an extra turn

48

49

50
You score the winner against Finland in the new gaffer's first World Cup qualifier in charge!
Move to square 53

35
Disaster! A sneaky Argie shoves you, so you boot him and get sent-off. Everyone hates you!
Go back to square one

34

33

32

31

26

27
The gaffer says you're not focused and leaves you out of the team
Go back to square 15

28

29
On from the start against Colombia, you score a great free-kick
Move to square 33

30

15

14

13
England lose at home to Italy and vital qualification points are dropped
Go back to square 10

12

11

6

7

8
The boss keeps playing you out of position at right wing-back
Miss your next turn

9

10

THE BIG MATCH QUIZ
ANSWERS

Right, here's where we identify the real footy fans from the wannabes, where we separate the budding stattos from the mere armchair fans! The moment of truth is upon us, as you check off your scores to find what kind of trophy you're worthy of. So do you deserve a World Cup winners' medal or a free transfer? Total up your score and find out!

261-300
YOU'VE WON THE WORLD CUP!

A star in the making! Anything over the 261 mark rates as a very special footy brain. You must go to every game and your head's pretty much a portable footy encyclopedia. Watch out, all your mates are gonna be after you for the latest info!

221-260
YOU'VE WON THE CHAMPIONS LEAGUE!

A top performance! Okay, so you haven't claimed footy's top prize, but you've shown you've got well above the normal amount of talent. Just a bit of hard work and more reading of MATCH, and you should be at the pinnacle!

176-220
YOU'VE WON THE FA CUP!

You deserve credit! A solid showing that marks you out as well worthy of a mention, but you may have had a little bit of luck on the way. Don't give up though, because anyone that can claim the FA Cup is still special!

131-175
YOU'VE WON THE LEAGUE CUP!

Good, but not brilliant! Okay, so it's still silverware, but you've really got to be aiming higher than this. You need a bit of polishing up on your footy facts to get the big, prestigious trophies. Keep at it though – and you never know!

86-130
YOU'VE WON THE SECOND DIVISION!

Oh dear! You have to admit this isn't anything special. The only positive to take out of this is that you still have the hope to go further, but that's about it! This is going to be a real test of your character, because you need to work!

41-85
YOU'VE WON THE LDV VANS TROPHY!

Oh well, you had a nice day out! Let's face it, no-one really cares about the LDV do they? It's the bargain basement consolation prize for you, we're afraid. Keep at it, but we're not holding out much hope. You must try harder!

under 40
YOU'VE WON A FREE TRANSFER!

You're out of here! Too bad. You had your chance, but too many easy errors spelled the end for you. We can't work out why you attempted it in the first place. Under 40 is, quite frankly, woeful – you need to read MATCH much more!

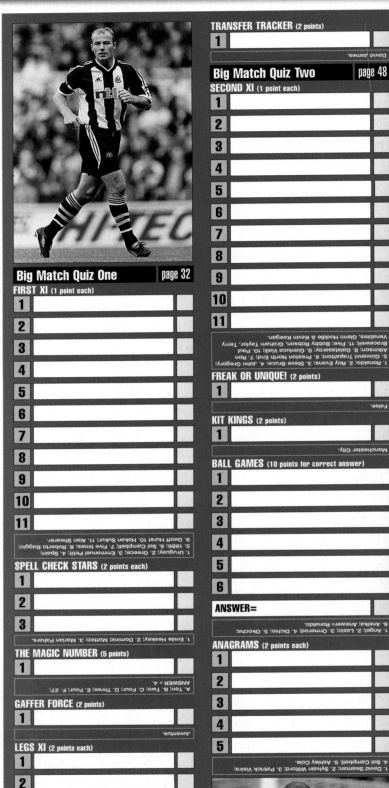

Big Match Quiz One   page 32

FIRST XI (1 point each)
1.
2.
3.
4.
5.
6.
7.
8.
9.
10.
11.

1. Uruguay; 2. Greece; 3. Emmanuel Petit; 4. Spain; 5. 1986; 6. Sol Campbell; 7. Five times; 8. Roberto Baggio; 9. Geoff Hurst 10. Hakan Sukur, 11. Alan Shearer.

SPELL CHECK STARS (2 points each)
1.
2.
3.

1. Emile Heskey; 2. Dominic Matteo; 3. Marian Pahars.

THE MAGIC NUMBER (5 points)
1.

A. Ten; B. Two; C. Four; D. Three; E. Four; F. 27; ANSWER = 4.

GAFFER FORCE (2 points)
1.

Juventus.

LEGS XI (2 points each)
1.
2.

1. David Dunn 2. Frank Lampard.

ROBERT PIRES QUIZ (2 points each)
1.
2.
3.
4.
5.

1. Marseille; 2. £6m; 3. True; 4. Aston Villa; 5. Newcastle.

TRANSFER TRACKER (2 points)
1.

David James.

Big Match Quiz Two   page 48

SECOND XI (1 point each)
1.
2.
3.
4.
5.
6.
7.
8.
9.
10.
11.

1. Ronaldo; 2. Roy Evans; 3. Steve Bruce; 4. John Gregory; 5. Giovanni Trapattoni; 6. Preston North End; 7. Ron Atkinson; 8. Galatasaray; 9. Gianluca Vialli; 10. Paul Bracewell; 11. Five: Bobby Robson, Graham Taylor, Terry Venables, Glenn Hoddle & Kevin Keegan.

FREAK OR UNIQUE! (2 points)
1.

False.

KIT KINGS (2 points)
1.

Manchester City.

BALL GAMES (10 points for correct answer)
1.
2.
3.
4.
5.
6.

ANSWER =

1. Angel; 2. Lazio; 3. Ormerod; 4. Dichio; 5. Okocha; 6. Anelka; Answer= Ronaldo.

ANAGRAMS (2 points each)
1.
2.
3.
4.
5.

1. David Seaman; 2. Sylvain Wiltord; 3. Patrick Vieira; 4. Sol Campbell; 5. Ashley Cole.

AND SEE HOW YOU HAVE SCORED!

THOSE WERE THE DAYS (3 points)

1 [ ]

Gianfranco Zola.

SPELL CHECK STARS (2 points)

1 [ ]
2 [ ]
3 [ ]
4 [ ]
5 [ ]

1. Nicolas Anelka; 2. Junichi Inamoto; 3. El Hadji Diouf; 4. Dele Adebola; 5. Marcus Allback.

SAY WHAT? (2 points)

1 [ ]

Ronaldo.

EYE EYE (2 points each)

1 [ ]
2 [ ]
3 [ ]
4 [ ]
5 [ ]

1. Simon Davies; 2. Ugo Ehiogu; 3. Craig Bellamy; 4. Alan Smith; 5. David Dunn.

Big Match Quiz Three page 58

THIRD XI (1 point each)

1 [ ]
2 [ ]
3 [ ]
4 [ ]
5 [ ]
6 [ ]
7 [ ]
8 [ ]
9 [ ]
10 [ ]
11 [ ]

1. Real Madrid; 2. False - Liverpool have won it four times; 3. Juventus; 4. 2000 & 2001; 5. a) 2; 6. UEFA Cup; 7. True - 1979 & 1980; 8. ITV; 9. b) 3; 10. 1999; 11. Bayern Munich.

CAP IN HAND (3 points)

1 [ ]

c) 73.

ALPHABET QUIZ (2 points each)

1 [ ]
2 [ ]
3 [ ]
4 [ ]
5 [ ]

1. Holland; 2. Helguera; 3. Hampden Park; 4. Heskey; 5. Hargreaves.

WHO AM I? (2 points)

1 [ ]

Nick Chadwick.

GOALMOUTH SCRAMBLE (Maximum 15 points)

[ ]

Car, card, chair, had, hair, hard, has, hid, raid, rich, nd, sad, shard, sir.

STEVEN GERRARD QUIZ (2 points each)

1 [ ]
2 [ ]
3 [ ]
4 [ ]
5 [ ]

1. 22 years old; 2. True; 3. a); 1998; 4. Ukraine; 5. Four.

TRANSFER TRACKER (3 points)

1 [ ]

Marcel Desailly.

SPELL CHECK STARS (2 points each)

1 [ ]
2 [ ]
3 [ ]

1. Hernan Crespo; 2. Rivaldo; 3. Filippo Inzaghi.

Big Match Quiz Four page 74

FOURTH XI (1 point each)

1 [ ]
2 [ ]
3 [ ]
4 [ ]
5 [ ]
6 [ ]
7 [ ]

1. David Beckham; 2. Roy Keane; 3. Rio Ferdinand; 4. Sylvain Legwinski.

---

8 [ ]
9 [ ]
10 [ ]
11 [ ]

1. Manchester United; 2. Sir Alex Ferguson; 3. Alan Shearer; 4. He scored his 200th Premiership goal; 5. It was the first time United hadn't finished in the top two; 6. 75 points; 7. Crystal Palace, Middlesbrough & Nottingham Forest; 8. True; 9. Ledley King (after just ten seconds v Bradford in Dec 2000); 10. Ipswich; 11. Chelsea.

BALL GAMES (10 points for correct answer)

1 [ ]
2 [ ]
3 [ ]
4 [ ]
5 [ ]
6 [ ]

ANSWER= [ ]

1. Carlos; 2. Southgate; 3. Everton; 4. New York; 5. Kilbane; 6. Eric; Answer: Henry.

GAFFER FORCE (2 points)

1 [ ]

South Korea.

ALAN SHEARER QUIZ (2 points each)

1 [ ]
2 [ ]
3 [ ]
4 [ ]
5 [ ]

1. True; 2. France; 3. Five; 4. £15 million; 5. Blackburn.

ONE OF A KIND (3 points)

1 [ ]

Lauren.

ANAGRAMS (2 points each)

1 [ ]
2 [ ]
3 [ ]
4 [ ]
5 [ ]

1. Emile Heskey; 2. Ruud van Nistelrooy; 3. Patrick Vieira; 4. Paul Scholes; 5. Dwight Yorke.

WEIRD BEARDS (3 points each)

1 [ ]
2 [ ]
3 [ ]
4 [ ]

FREAK OR UNIQUE! (2 points)

1 [ ]

False.

Big Match Quiz Five page 88

FIFTH XI (1 point each)

1 [ ]
2 [ ]
3 [ ]
4 [ ]
5 [ ]
6 [ ]
7 [ ]
8 [ ]
9 [ ]
10 [ ]
11 [ ]

1. Seven points clear; 2. Thierry Henry; 3. True - 4-0; 4. Three - David Seaman, Richard Wright & Stuart Taylor; 5. The lucky north dressing room; 6. Ray Parlour; 7. Freddie Ljungberg; 8. b) nine goals; 9. True; 10. Sylvain Wiltord; 11. 1998.

GROUND FORCE (1 point)

1 [ ]

Goodison Park (Everton).

ONE OF A KIND (2 points)

1 [ ]

Zidane.

FREAK OR UNIQUE! (2 points)

1 [ ]

False.

LEGS XI (2 points each)

1 [ ]
2 [ ]

1. Marcel Desailly; 2. Roy Keane.

SAY WHAT? (2 points)

1 [ ]

Michael Owen.

WHO AM I? (2 points)

1 [ ]

Craig Bellamy.

WORD FIT – BIG MATCH QUIZ 1

Out of 20 points I scored...

MEGA WORDSPOT – BIG MATCH QUIZ 5

Out of 36 points I scored...

FOOTY

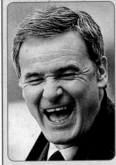

JOKES!

Impress your pals with these gags...

FAMOUS UNITED FAN!

> "I was standing outside Old Trafford and 300 fans ran at me, yelling for my autograph," says one fan. "I don't believe you," says his mate. "It's true," the fan replies, "ask David Beckham – he was right next to me at the time!"

BOOBY BORO!

> Why are Middlesbrough like a dodgy old bra?
> *Because they've got no cups and little support!*

LYIN' REFEREES!

> At the Referees Annual Dinner Dance, three guys turn up at the entrance. "Where are your tickets?" asks the bouncer. "We don't need tickets, we're friends with one of the refs," replies one of the men. The bouncer looks puzzled, and says: "I don't believe that. A ref would never have three friends!"

CHEEKY NIPPER!

> After a Liverpool game, a kid asks Emile Heskey for his autograph. Next match, the same kid asks for his autograph again. This happens for the next three games, until Emile says, "Look, I've given you my autograph five times – what's up?" The kid smiles and says, "Five more from you and I can swap for one of Michael Owen's!"

LITTLE TRACTOR BOY!

> The seven dwarves are working down the mine when there's a cave-in. Snow White runs to the entrance and yells down to them. In the distance, a voice shouts "Ipswich Town for the FA Cup!" So Snow White says, "Well, at least Dopey's still alive!"

11 ESSENTIAL SIGNS

...that you've turned into an absolute football nut case!

1 On matchdays with a 3pm kick-off, you arrive at the ground at five in the morning! Armed with your huge autograph book and camera, you wait for ten hours before the game actually starts!

2 For your favourite player's birthday, you bake him a cake and take it to the training ground, along with a card and prezzie – even though it's a school day!

3 You demand a rise in your pocket money. When it's refused, you go on strike and instruct your agent to find new parents. You get a nice Italian couple and receive 200 million Lira per week!

4 Even in July, your Motty-style sheepskin stays on. You smell like a dead fish and look a right wally, using a hairbrush to commentate on games!

5 Every throw-in your team wins in the campaign is marked on your special 'throw-in graph'. At the end of the season, you send the manager a 'throw-in report' on every player. Very interesting!

6 The fittest girl in school asks you out to the pictures, but you stay in to watch the Bulgarian League highlights on Eurosport. Your best mate gets to take the bird out instead, you muppet!

7 Anxious to see the weekend's results unfold, you sit two inches away from the TV from Tuesday onwards and stare stupidly at Teletext. Nobody is allowed to watch Neighbours and your eyes eventually pop out of their sockets!

8 When a new footy boot comes out, you flog your granny's best china just to get them and she has to drink her tea out of flowerpots. You don't care one bit, saying it'll help her poor knees!

9 You grow a David Seaman ponytail and stick on a fake moustache. The headmaster threatens to expel you, so you do a 'Danny Mills' and decide to shave all your hair off. You still get expelled. Doh!

10 When your mum says you can't have chips for tea, you go into a Paolo di Canio rage – waving your arms and ranting in Italian at her. You vow never to clean up your room again!

11 You're such a football nut that you demand a job writing for MATCH. It's a dream position, because you're soon surrounded by other odd-looking weirdos who also talk about footy all day long!

Wow, is that another year of footy over already? We hope you've enjoyed this year's MATCH annual. Now that you've tested yourself on the quizzes, caught up on all the goss, and read about how the Premiership's Super Strikers made it to the top, it's time to look forward. Last season might have been the most exciting in years, but we've got high hopes for this 2002-03 campaign! Remember, you can keep up-to-date with all the latest news, top interviews and star posters in your weekly copy of MATCH magazine – in the shops every Tuesday! But if you've got any ideas for the 2004 annual, you can contact us at this address: 2004 Annual Suggestions, MATCH Towers, Bushfield House, Orton Centre, Peterborough, PE2 5UW. See ya!